Tourism and World Trade Organisation

Tourism and World Trade Organisation

By

Dr. M. Lakshmi Narasaiah
M.A., Ph.D.

Professor of Economics,
Co-ordinator, Department of M.B.A. and Commerce,
Special Officer,
Sri Krishnadevaraya University Post-graduate Centre,
Kurnool–518 002
Andhra Pradesh (India)

DISCOVERY PUBLISHING HOUSE
NEW DELHI

Reprinted – 2025

ISBN: 978-81-8356-080-1

Tourism and World Trade Organisation

Published by:
DISCOVERY PUBLISHING HOUSE
4383/4B, Ansari Road, Darya Ganj
New Delhi-110 002 (India)
Phone: +91-11-23279245; 23253475; 43596065
Mobile: +91 9811179893 / +91 9871656464
E-mail: discoverybooksindia@gmail.com
orderdphbooks@gmail.com
namitwasan9@gmail.com
web: www.discoverypublishinggroup.com

Printed at:
Infinity Imaging Systems
Delhi

Preface

The reason why trade has such a vital part to play in building peace is because it means lowering barriers—not only to goods and services but among nations and peoples. The elimination of barriers creates interdependence and interdependence creates solidarity. The history of the last fifty years has shown us all the undeniable benefits of lowering trade barriers and opening economies.

Clearly every region has its own characteristics, and it would be wrong to imagine that the same blueprint can apply everywhere and in the same way. Any region which was for thousands of years at the crossroads of world trade should regain its place in the centre, because doing so will help build peace as well as prosperity. This is why the numerous applications for accession to the WTO from various countries are so significant. The first is through regionalism. There are several efforts at regional trade and economic initiatives among countries, and that such initiatives will be encouraged to reduce positive results. Regional initiatives are important because they can help countries at a comparable level of development to move relatively quickly in opening their economies and in deepening their interdependence.

However, the rapid advance of global economic integration means that while regional initiatives remain important, they are not sufficient by themselves to address successfully the new perspectives of the international economy. That is why there is a need for second track, which is the rule-based multilateral system. And that is why the multilateral system is of fundamental importance to the economic prosperity of any region.

As the first major international institution to be created in the post-cold war era, the WTO offers a promise of the kind of global economic architecture which need in the coming decades. Its culture is firmly rooted in the tradition of consensus-building and cooperation among sovereign countries. And the WTO embodies rights and obligations negotiated by consensus, approved and ratified by each government and each parliament, and they are enforceable, not through the crude exercise of economic power, but through the rule of law. The alternative would be a power-based system—who would want to chose this option?

But most importantly the WTO is an organisation which brings all countries—from all corners of the world and from all levels of development—together as equals. There is no weighted voting, no exclusive clubs, no inner and outer circles. Developing countries representing 80 per cent of constituency sit as equals with industrialized countries to write the rules of a shared trading system.

This new unity of developing and developed countries inside a single system will be credited as the greatest achievement of the multilateral system. But this unity is still fragile: we cannot allow it to be broken. This is why, in preparing the agenda of the first Ministerial meeting in Singapore, have recognized the particularly difficult task facing developing countries in implementing the Uruguay Round Commitments. They have also acknowledged the challenges they face in contemplating the necessary work programme.

The integration of developing countries as equal partners in the multilateral system is one of the most important challenges in shaping the economic order of the 21st century. This is a shared responsibility of developed and developing countries alike. There is no rational alternative to this objective. The evolution of the global economy makes that clear.

Now there is a need to work together as equal partners to ensure the full integration, and all other developing and transition economies, into the global economy and the rule-based multilateral trading system. In conjunction with this there is a need to encourage, notably the growth of regional economic cooperation. The alternative is a vicious circle where economic isolation feeds greater political instability which in turn leads to greater economic isolation. The road to a lasting peace in the world begins, not ends, with economic integration and interdependence. Taking this message to heart will help build a future where its goods, services, and investment that cross borders—not missiles and soldiers.

Dr. M. Lakshmi Narasaiah

Contents

1

Sustainable Tourism Development

Tourism has grown into one of the world's major industries and has thus also become an increasingly important, if complex, issue for environmental policy. Unless it is developed in a sustainable manner, we will be unable to achieve key objectives of global environmental policy such as the preservation of biological diversity, the prevention of climate change or the conservation of natural resources.

Tourism itself depends a lot on the existence of unspoilt nature and landscapes, as well as a healthy environment. If nature is plundered, landscapes are destroyed or water, energy and soil resources are over-exploited, the economic basis of tourism is also undermined. The needs of tourism do therefore overlap with those of environmental protection and nature conservation.

On the one hand, for instance, tourists are becoming increasingly environmentally conscious and are looking to get back to nature and enjoy unspoilt environments when on holiday. On the other hand, however, the number of international tourists is growing constantly. The proportion of long-haul journeys is also increasing steadily, especially in the industrialised nations, where travel is now taken for granted as part of people's lifestyles and has become an important factor in social status. The many different types of travel and holidays are covering more and more countries and regions and, as a result, increasing numbers of previously unspoilt natural environments are being opened up to tourism. This applies equally to coastlines, small islands, coral reefs, rock formations and mountain regions.

There is growing recognition of the need for tourism to develop in a sustainable and environmentally friendly manner. Many countries have, for instance, introduced regulations which require environmental impact surveys to be carried out at least for larger tourist developments. Since the Rio Summit in 1992, there have also been more initiatives in support of sustainable tourism at international level.

- Sustainable tourism allows for the rational use of biological diversity and can contribute to the preservation of that diversity.
- The development of tourism must be controlled and carefully managed so that it remains sustainable.
- Particular attention must be paid to tourism in ecologically and culturally sensitive areas, where mass tourism should be avoided.
- All parties concerned, including in particular the private sector, have a part to play in bringing about the sustainable development of tourism, and voluntary initiatives (codes of conduct, quality labels) should be encouraged.
- Particular importance should be attached to the local level, which is not only responsible for the sustainable development of tourism but should also derive particular benefit from tourism.

It will mark the successful beginning of internationally co-ordinated efforts to make tourism environmentally and socially sustainable so that many generations to come can continue to experience and enjoy the beauty of nature on our planet.

2

Sustainable Tourism—Illusion or Realistic Alternative?

We find them in the big cities of the world and in the most remote jungles; they cross the deserts of Africa and cruise to see the penguins along the polar ice caps: they climb the Himalayan mountains and dive deep into the coral seas of tropical oceans. Tourists are every where these days—easily recognisable by their cameras and camcorders, their leisure-time outfit, and their unsatiable desire to get away from home and experience life with a difference.

Tourism has become the biggest industry in the world. It offers jobs for 200 million people and contributes 11.7 per cent to global Gross National Product. Almost 700 million tourist arrivals are expected for this year, and this number is estimated to grow to 1.5 billion by the year 2020.

Most countries in the world, with very few exceptions, compete with each other to get as large a share as possible of the huge cake which is up for distribution. Attracting tourists, especially from beyond the own borders, means foreign exchange earnings and jobs and income for the local people. But the list of possible drawbacks, especially for developing countries, is along the environment and natural beauty may be harmed by infrastructure and hotel buildings; the intrusion of large numbers of foreigners with little knowledge and respect for the local culture and tradition may cause social tensions; there may be an upsurge of prostitution and sex-related diseases; and the local economy may be disrupted because labour is siphoned off from farming to the tourism sector, and the high purchasing power of tourists may promote inflation.

People concerned over these undesirable side-effects of tourism have, therefore, invented the term of 'soft' tourism—one which would impact less on the society and environment of the host country. The latest catchwords are 'sustainable' tourism or 'eco-tourism' suggesting that tourism can be organised in such a way that it does not harm the environment and local culture. But are we not deceiving ourselves if we believe that tourism in its modern forms can be 'sustainable'? Sustainable according to the widely used definition of the Brundtlandt Commission means "meeting the needs of the present without compromising the ability of future generations to meet their own needs".

This entails, for instance, that we try to avoid the possible effects of climate change which is caused by greenhouse gas emissions into the atmosphere. Tourism, because of the enormous increase in air and road traffic, is a major factor in polluting the atmosphere, increasing CO_2 emissions, and damaging the protective ozone layer. Also, increased traffic as a result of tourism used up additional non-renewal resources such as petrol and kerosene and adds to air pollution in overcrowded cities or in frequented tourist regions. Needless to argue that the term 'sustainable' could hardly be applied in this connection, especially in view of that fact that tourist numbers are going to double in the next 20 years.

Also tourism is by no means more 'sustainable' if tourist leave their ghettos and begin to interact with the local population. As long as only a few open-minded people seek to submerge themselves in the culture and society of the host country this may lead to more interaction and inter-cultural understanding. But just imagine what would happen if all the Japanese and Americans visiting Paris, Rome or Berlin during the summer would come knocking at the door of local people to learn more about their real life. Or if all the Germans on the beaches of Thailand would decide that travelling with a backpack through the country's villages was more rewarding than staying in a luxurious hotel. Then it would soon turn out that such a form of tourism was even less 'sustainable' than organised travel in its present form.

The only truly 'sustainable' form of tourism, therefore, would be to stay at home and to avoid additional resource consumption. For obvious reasons, this is no realistic alternative and, if consistently applied, would lead to a world economic crisis. Instead of using the illusionary term 'sustainable' tourism, we should, therefore, speak more often about 'responsible' tourism. This term implies that we try to keep the negative environmental and cultural impacts of tourism at a minimum while making sure that benefits go to the poor, especially in developing countries. 'Responsible' tourism is not against travelling, but it takes care that landscapes are not destroyed, natural and architectural beauties preserved, foreign cultures respected, and economic benefits spread as widely as possible. 'Responsible' tourism has the advantage that corresponds both to the wishes of most tourists who want to stay in a clean environment with a clean conscience and the interests of the local people who derive jobs and incomes from it. But it needs a strong state which is able to enforce environmental regulations, suppress corruption and make sure that income from tourism benefits the whole country and not only a few national or international entrepreneurs.

To travel and to experience the world is an age-old dream which more and more people in the richer parts of the world are able to fulfil for themselves. But the tourism boom threatens to become self-destructive if it continues to expand without fetters. 'Responsible' tourism strikes a balance between the needs of the environment, the respect for the other culture, and the wish of modern people to live in a world without borders. However, it is an illusion to believe that mass tourism with 1.5 billion arrivals per year could truly be sustainable.

3

Sustainable Tourism and the Environment

Tourism is high on the international agenda. The 7th session of the Commission on Sustainable Development focused on tourism and subsequently work programmes on sustainable tourism are being developed. Also the Convention on Biological Diversity is embarking on tourism programmes and bilateral and multilateral financial institutions placed tourism high on their priority lists. The UN declared 2002 as the International Year of Ecotourism and the World Tourism Organisation adopted a Global Code of Ethics for Tourism at its General Assembly, held in Santiago de Chile.

The World Tourism Organisation forecasts that there will be 702 million international arrivals in the year 2002, that arrivals will top one billion in the year 2010 and that by 2020 international arrivals will reach 1.6 billion—nearly three times the number of international trips made in 1996, which was 592 million.

Travellers of the 21st century will go farther and farther. The Tourism 2020 Vision forecast predicts that by 2020 one out of every three trips will be a long-haul journey to another region of the world. It is expected that China will become a major force in international tourism and the WTO predicts that about 100 million Chinese will take international trips by 2020, thus putting them in fourth place in numbers of travellers after Germany, Japan and the United States. By the same time,

China will attract 137 million visitors—63.5 million overseas visitors travelled to China in 1998 and thus outrank France as the world's top destination. It is estimated that during 1999 France will receive a record number of tourists of more than 70 million; in 2007 France hopes to attract 90 million visitors. The key resource for the most popular tourist destinations is the natural environment: coastal resorts, tropical rainforests, wildlife in national parks and alpine skiresorts, all rely on a mixture of natural beauty, good weather and safe conditions to attract holiday destination is landscape and natural environment, followed by climate, the cost of the journey and the historical features of the place to visit. Hence, conserving the ecological integrity and environment is imperative if tourism is to be sustained.

The pressure from millions of tourists on water and marine resources, on land and landscape, on wildlife and habitat is enormous and often has devastating impact on the environment and the local population who are increasingly deprived of access to clean water and other natural resources.

In some regions, particularly in small island countries, tourism is one of the major reasons for wasting and polluting water: on average one tourist consumes at least 6 times more water than a local resident.

Major water wasters and polluters are golf courses. In many countries, golf has brought heavy ecological and social costs: deforestation, the destruction of bio-diversity and erosion; dispossession of peoples' homes and farms; over-consumption and pollution of water and very high use of pesticides and fertilisers which threaten local residents, workers, wildlife and the golfers themselves. A survey by the Japanese National Doctors' Health Insurance Association has revealed that many golfers, caddies and residents living near a golf course suffer from skin inflammation, disorders of the ear, nose and throat and other respiratory illnesses to the inhalation of pesticides because up to 90 per cent of the chemicals sprayed on golf courses end up in the air. In some areas in Thailand, diseases emerged which, prior to the construction of golf courses, had not been known.

In some regions, golf courses have depleted water supply, agricultural production has come to a halt, peasants have become impoverished and forced to migrate to urban areas in search of employment. Golf courses take large amounts of land. It is estimated that each year worldwide up to 5,000 hectares of forest are cut to clear land for golf courses.

Very often, the construction of golf courses forms an integral part of a comprehensive tourism project. Adjacent to the golf course condominiums and/or hotels are built, very often also a marina, an airport and a casino. Studies have shown that such a complex not only has touristic objective but is often connected to drug trafficking and money-laundering. Even the US State Department has emphasised the link between tourism, money-laundering and offshore banking.

Cruise ships are a major cause for pollution in the Caribbean, destroying maritime life and reefs by releasing waste into the ocean. Recently the Royal Caribbean, the world's second largest cruise line was fined a record sum of US $18 million for dumping waste oil and hazardous chemicals into the sea. The company admitted to routinely dumping wasted oil from its fleet and that it deliberately dumped in U.S. harbours and coastal areas many other types of pollutants, including hazardous chemicals from photo processing equipment, dry cleaning shops and printing presses. Some hazardous materials, including toxic solvents from dry cleaning operations, were illegally placed in the garbage aboard the ships. The material was then either incinerated on the ship or dumped in U.S. or foreign ports mixed with ordinary garbage.

It was announced that the Royal Caribbean Cruise reported a profit of US $338 million in 1997, a 93 per cent increase over the previous year, Carnival Corporation's Holland, the biggest cruise company with a turnover of

US $3 billion in 1997 made a net profit of US $836 million, 25 per cent more than in 1996. Both cruise companies have recently been fined millions of dollars for dumping untreated bilge water, oil and other waste into Alaskan waters.

However, the impact of oil and hazardous waste on water, maritime life and coral reefs is devastating and all fines paid for the damage caused by the cruise ships will not revive dead corals.

A recent Green Peace study on coral reefs—one of the marine world's great natural treasures—predicts that the coral bleaching which dramatically whitened many of the world's reefs last year will escalate rapidly under accepted global climate models and that the damage would wreak havoc in fisheries and tourism, disrupting the economies of many nations.

A WWF study recently published on "Climate Change and its Impacts on Tourism", warned that droughts, rising seas, flash floods, forest fires and diseases could turn profitable destinations into holiday horror stories. The report urges the tourist industry to persuade western industrialised governments to take more concerted action to reduce their nations' carbon-di-oxide emissions, the main cause of global warming.

The Need for Action and Education

If governments, the international community and the tourism industry want to save the world's major tourist destinations, immediate action is required. Governments and the tourism industry must abide to the principle that environmental protection is an integral part of tourism development. In order to protect the environment and mitigate the damages caused by tourism, some countries have decided to take action: The Spanish Island Minorca and the Seychelles will introduce Eco-tax on tourism. This tax will be around.

US $12 per person in Minorca and its revenues are earmarked for the maintenance of national parks and the restoration of damaged coastline. Visitors to the Seychelles will have to buy a so-called "gold-card" at a price of 100 $ which entitles unlimited access to the country; income from this card will be used for sewage management and protection of fresh water supply.

Only if tourism investors and developers:

(*a*) consider the natural capacity for the regeneration and future productivity of natural resources.

(*b*) recognise the contribution that people and communities, customs and lifestyles, make to the tourism experience and therefore accept that these people must have an equitable share in the economic benefits of tourism; and

(*c*) listen to local people in the tourist destinations, tourism may become sustainable.

Education and awareness raising campaigns at all levels are therefore imperative.

4

The Tourism Juggernaut

Tourism, already one of the world's biggest industries, is expected to treble in size by the year 2010. Now, concern about tourism's impact on fragile environments and cultures is leading to serious attempts to make it more 'sustainable'.

"Getting away from it all," is understandably popular. With so many wonderful places in the world, prices of international travel falling, and the stresses and strains of everyday life increasing, more people are travelling

"The sustained growth since the beginning of this decade and the acceleration now underway proves that tourism is one of the world's most durable and dynamic economic sectors." But around every silver lining, there is always a cloud, and as tourism grows, so too do the criticisms. Evidence of the downside of tourism—culturally, environmentally and economically—is now such that tourism has become a dirty word amongst many communities, environmental groups, and human rights campaigners.

Tourism's vociferous appetite for basic resources—land, water and energy—has meant that the tourism industry and governments are increasingly finding themselves opposed over land rights and water rights by local people. One of the most famous long-term tourism protests has been in Goa. With one five-star hotel consuming as much water as five local villages and one five-star tourist consuming 28 times more electricity per day than a local Goan, local discontent over resource-use is understandable.

Lack of access by locals to public beaches, violation by hotels of environmental regulations, and heavy-handed tactics by local authorities to free-up beach areas for hotel's use, have all been cited in legal disputes throughout the world. Commercialisation of culture and destruction of traditional lifestyles also became commonplace.

Tourism is also cited in terms of gross human rights abuse. In Burma, the military junta has forcibly moved millions of people from their homes to make room for tourism development, and used hundreds of thousands as forced labour on tourism-related projects. Such problems are often brushed aside by the tourism industry and by governments, who cite the economic bonuses behind promoting tourism.

But as foreign exchange leakages from developing to developed countries equal around 60 to 75 per cent, and local jobs are generally menial and low-paid, the economic benefits are often skewed away from destination countries. This is particularly the case in destinations which receive a lot of cheap, package tours.

Sustainable tourism is defined as: "Tourism and associated infrastructures that operate within capacities for the regeneration and future productivity of natural resources, recognise the contribution of local people and their cultures, accept that these people must have an equitable share in the economic benefits of tourism, and are guided by the wishes of local people and communities in the destination areas."

Such a definition seems reasonable, but as with the 'sustainable development' of any industry—to implement it is more difficult, particularly in developing countries. How can a country set limits on the numbers of tourists it accepts when it desperately needs foreign exchange to pay off foreign debts and fuel economic growth? How can local people receive an equitable share of tourism's profits when there is no way they can compete with the foreign multinational hotels and tour operators on price, and do not have the same international marketing networks? And how can developers be forced to consult with a representative sample of local people, and not just the business elite?

At the nub of sustainable tourism are issues of equity and local control-issues that it is almost impossible for the tourism industry to address because of their need to maximise profit. Changes are occurring, but they tend to be in simpler areas such as environmental management. Efforts are being made by the hotel industry for instance, to encourage responsible water, waste and energy management, which includes a wide range of techniques including extensive recycling, water and energy conservation and uses of alternative energy, such as solar power.

5

Ecotourism or Ecocide?

Ecotourism is the fastest growing part of the world travel business, but whether it destroys more than it protects will depend upon how it is put into practice.

For the travel and tourism industry, ecotourism is the fastest growing 'market segment', generally equated with nature tourism. Interpreted merely as a product, however, it may be ecologically based but not ecologically sound, responsible or sustainable.

To incorporate these vital characteristics ecotourism must adhere to three essential principles: The first is, perhaps, the most obvious. As an industry based on the beauty and diversity of nature, it is evident that it should not deplete or degrade those resources and thus prejudice its own future. Ecotourism must, therefore, be ecologically sound, requiring a two-way link between itself and environmental conservation.

To consider nature without recognising the link with people will, however, compromise sustainability. It is now widely recognised that conservation cannot be divorced from development issues. The second principle is therefore that ecotourism must be responsible, paying regard to local needs and improving local welfare.

However, to be truly sustainable, ecotourism needs to fulfill the ambitions and expectations of all interests. The third principle, then, is to consider not only the interests of tourism enterprises and organisations, but also visitor satisfaction, the needs of tourists.

If, ecotourism embodies these essential principles, symbiotic relationships between the varying interests should follow, with environmental protection resulting both from and in enhanced standards of living for local populations, continued profits for the tourism industry, sustained visitor attraction, and revenue for conservation. An examination of ecotourism across these dimensions, highlights not only its potential but also its problems.

Local Benefits

The high ground claimed by ecotourism, in terms of its contribution to development, is that, in principle, it offers enhanced prospects for local involvement compared with conventional tourism. As well a moral obligation to incorporate the local people in projects that affect them, such incorporation has important developmental implications.

Tourism income may be captured locally through revenue sharing schemes, through entrepreneurship and labour, and through the sale of tourist merchandise. Tourism can also act as a catalyst, and even provide some of the finance, for the improvement of essential services such as clean water, sanitation, electricity supply and transport. It may also provide an incentive for improved education and skills and the potential for participation in decision-making.

Local involvement also makes sense for conserving natural environments. It has been recognised that, as people realise the benefits from ecotourism, support for conservation increases. Ecotourism may also provide the incentive for the survival of a traditional culture. The cultural and the natural are often inextricably linked to form the composite attraction of a particular ecotourism destination. The terracing of the Himalayan foothills, the hot springs at Tatopani, Sikkim are all examples of the fusion of the natural and the cultural.

Greater local involvement makes practical sense for national and local governments, agencies and operators using local labour, expertise and knowledge. Education is a two-way process, improved understanding of local circumstances is likely to increase project efficiency. Building upon local experience and traditions provides a foundation for wise and successful development, and, simultaneously, an ecotourism asset.

Introduction to indigenous uses of natural products also broadens the base of environmental interpretation. Local involvement is not without its problems, however. Revenue sharing schemes may neither benefit the most needy, nor those most adversely affected. Beneficiaries may often be passive recipients, rather than active participants. The emphasis must be on participation rather than patronisation, if traditional livelihood are removed they must be replaced with others.

Local participation, however, often consists of employment rather than entrepreneurship, where constraints of costs of entry, language, education and skills operate. Furthermore, the nature of local employment tends to be low skilled, poorly paid and often seasonal. The higher status, better paid jobs, particularly managerial positions, tend to be occupied by outsiders.

Industry Profits

The integrity of the tourism 'product' is vital to the interests of tourism entrepreneurs, and all those who are associated with them, such as tourist boards, government departments, NGO's and international aid agencies. Tourism operators benefit from public support, increased credibility and demand for associated products. Sound environmental practice often makes good business sense.

There are, however, many practical and institutional obstacles to effective ecotourism management, not the least of which will be the problems of vested interests who are more concerned with short-term profits than with the long-term.

Pressure of Numbers

Another dilemma is the sheer problem of numbers. To confine attention, however, to the consideration of small-scale, more easily managed ecotourism projects, involving small specialist groups paying high prices, is to invite ecocide at higher levels.

Rapid growth rates imply inevitable change. Psychological carrying capacity (as well as other types of carrying capacity) will probably be breached and visitor satisfaction compromised. This is especially true when visitors are concentrated in space and time.

However much a principled definition of ecotourism is advocated, it must be recognised that so-called ecotourists are not an homogeneous group. The spectrum of participants embraces hard-core nature tourists through to casual day visitors. Their behaviour and consequent impact will vary accordingly. It is essential, therefore, to attempt to match numbers and types of ecotourists with destination characteristics.

Paying for Conservation

Willingness-to-pay surveys of ecotourists across the globe show a consistent response of $10 as reasonable visitor's fee. Certain unique sites, or those harbouring more charismatic species, can support higher fees. The potential revenue for conservation is therefore evident, but often not realised.

Where the fee falls below the amount visitors are willing to pay, the capability to contribute more fully towards conservation remains latent. It is also necessary to ensure that a proportion of revenues accrues locally. Percentages of revenues directed towards conservation vary between sites. Often high proportions end up in central treasuries.

The Challenge

The major role players in ecotourism all have a stake in its sustainable development. Their present and future interests are, in many ways, tied to one another. Given the multitude, and diversity, of stakeholders a completely sustainable outcome is, however, likely to remain elusive.

The grand challenge is to reconcile sometimes complementary, but often conflicting interests. The essential dilemma is to balance demands of ever-increasing 'new-tourists' escaping from the confines and pressures of urban life, and reacting against the characteristics of mass tourism with the needs of the environment, the aspirations of tourism organisations, and, most importantly, the basic needs of the local population.

Although a win-win scenario, where all interests gain, is the ideal outcome, there will often be situations where one interest may gain at the expense of another. National Parks, for example, may bring benefits for conservation and for visitors, but the local population is likely to lose out if they are excluded from their traditional activities.

The situation is fraught with discontinuities. A win situation for one interest in a particular place at a specific point in time is likely to be a loss for another. It is necessary, therefore, to recognise conflicts and identify relative costs and benefits. Arriving at the most sustainable outcome is likely to involve trade-offs. It is unlikely to be optimal either environmentally or developmentally, but, in the circumstances, it will be the most feasible and most practical. And, hopefully, ecocide will be circumvented.

6

The Biggest Industry the World Has Ever Seen

The Future of World Tourism

The year 2020 will see the penetration of technology into all aspects of life. It will become possible to live one's days without exposure to other people, according to WTO's latest look into the future.

But this bleak prognosis has a silver lining for the tourism sector. People in the high-tech future will crave the human touch and tourism will be the principal means to achieve this.

Tourism companies that manage to provide "high-touch" products will prosper. Upscale, luxury services that pamper and spoil their customers have a bright future in the upcoming century. But WTO's report also predicts good prospects for low-budget destinations and packages. Self-catering holiday facilities, for example, which offer plenty of opportunities for socialising among families and friends. Opportunities abound at both ends of the spectrum and there will be plenty of them.

$5 Billion a Day Industry

WTO's Study Tourism: 2020 Vision predicts 1.5 billion tourists will be visiting foreign countries annually by the year 2020, spending more than US $2 trillion or US $5 billion every day. These forecasts represent nearly three times more international tourists than the 66 million recorded in 1999 and nearly five times more tourism spending, which last year topped US $453 billion. Tourist arrivals are predicted to grow by an average 4.3 per cent a year over the next two decades, while receipts from international tourism will climb by 6.7 per cent a year.

To factor in domestic tourism, WTO multiplies arrivals by 10 and quadruples receipts, which brings us to the grant totals of 16 billion tourists spending US $8 trillion in 2020.

Tourism in the 21st century will not only be the world's biggest industry, it will be the largest by far that the world has ever seen. Along with its phenomenal growth and size, the tourism industry will also have to take on more responsibility for its extensive impacts. Not only its economic impact, but also its impact on the environment, on societies and on cultural sites, all of which will be increasingly scrutinised by governments, consumer groups and the travelling public.

We hope that Tourism 2020 Vision will be more than a useful marketing tool, that it will act as a warning signal for destinations—helping them recognise the need to prepare for the pressure of growth, WTO is advising destinations to implement long-term, strategic planning and to strengthen the partnerships, both strategically and at the operational level, between the public and private sectors.

Growth of Long-Haul

Tourism: 2020 Vision indicates that tourists of the 21st century will be travelling further afield on their holidays, often to China and even to outer space. The percentage of long-haul travel is predicted to increase from 18 per cent in 1995 to 24 per cent by 2020.

Tourism companies looking to cash in on this booming sector are advised to look towards Asia. China will be the world's number one destination by the year 2020 and it will also become the fourth most important generating market. Currently it does not even figure among the world's destinations predicted to make great strides in the tourism industry are Russia, Hong Kong, Thailand, Singapore, Indonesia and South Africa.

Short pleasure voyages to outer space will become a reality by 2004 or 2005, according to the study carried out by WTO Statistics Chief Enzo Paci in consultation with 85 governments and 50 tourism visionaries.

It is expected space trips will last up to four days and cost on average US $100,000. NASA, the US space agency, has recently surveyed the travel industry for interest in space tourism and some US companies are already taking reservations and deposits from private citizens hoping to become the first tourists in outer space.

But while some travellers may be suiting up for space voyages, the vast majority of the world's population will never leave their own countries, not even by the year 2020.

Only 7 per cent of the world's population will be travelling internationally by the year 2020, up from 3.5 per cent in 1996—but still just the tip of the iceberg.

European Trends

Tourism: 2020 Vision predicts that Europe will remain by far the leading inbound tourism region as well as the main generator of international tourists. International arrivals in Europe will reach 717 million by 2020, more than twice as many as last year.

Overall, tourism to Europe is predicted to grow more slowly than the world average; at a rate of 3.1 per cent annually, though some countries will fare better than others. Central and Eastern European countries will become the new motor for Europe, feeding and being fed by other European and long-haul generating markets. Tourism to Central and Eastern Europe will grow by 4.8 per cent a year and the former Soviet Block countries will surpass 200 million arrivals by 2016—a doubling in last 15 years.

The Eastern Mediterranean countries of Cyprus, Turkey and Israel are also expected to show good growth of 4.6 per cent a year. Tourism to the United Kingdom is forecast to grow by 4 per cent annually, just under the world average. Reflecting world patterns and increasing air travel, Europeans will be taking trips more frequently and further from home. Total outbound travel from European countries is predicted to reach 771 million trips a year by 2010, again more than twice as many as last year.

Long-haul travel to countries outside of Europe will grow by 6.1 per cent a year in the upcoming decades to reach 15 per cent of all trips taken by Europeans or 115,600,000 departures. Long-haul currently accounts for 12 per cent of European outbound travel or about 42 million trips a year.

Since the typical European tourist who spends his holiday at the beach will be more frequently choosing Asian or Caribean resorts, European beach destinations are advised to orientate their product development and marketing increasingly to new tourist sources, especially Japan, the newly industrialised countries of Asia and the Americas.

Mature European destinations will have continually to strive to seek product and market differentiation to avoid a tired or stale image in major generating markets.

Recipe for Success

While growth of the tourism industry will be unstoppable in the 21st century, increased benefits cannot be taken for granted. Competition among destinations will also become increasingly fierce.

The Study Tourism: 2020 Vision outlines a series of 12 megatrends that will shape the sector and offers advice on how to better compete. No destination or tourism operator can afford to sit back and wait for more tourists to arrive. They have to be won—and there will be winners and losers. To be a winner, there are a number of imperatives:

1. Development focused on quality and sustainability.

2. Value for money.

3. Full utilisation of information technology to identify and communicate effectively with market segments and niches.

Product development and marketing will need to match each other more closely, based on the main travel motivators of the 21st century. *Tourism: 2020 Vision* calls these motivating factors the Three E's—Entertainment, Excitement and Education.

The study also highlights the importance of image in a tourists' selection of a holiday destination in the future. While an image of safety and security is already an important deciding factor for tourists, holiday makers of the 21st century will be looking for places with a trendy image.

As 2020 Vision points out, the next century will mark the emergence of the tourism destinations as 'a fashion accessory'. The choice of holiday destination will help define the identity of the travellers and, in an increasingly homogeneous world, set him apart from the hordes of other tourists.

Boutique destinations and space agencies beware! You are on the threshold of meeting the 21st century tourist.

7

Pro-Poor Tourism

Opportunities for Sustainable Local Development

Tourism is the world's largest industry, with over 10 per cent of GDP globally directly related to tourism activities. Rising standards of living in the countries of the North, declining long-haul travel costs, increasing holiday entitlements, changing demographics and strong consumer demand for exotic international travel have resulted in significant tourism growth to developing countries. Tourism is the principal export for one-third of developing countries. Tourism brings relatively powerful consumers to Southern countries, potentially an important market for local entrepreneurs and an engine for local sustainable economic development. There is no reliable data on domestic tourism but it is growing rapidly in South America and in China and Southeast Asia; it represents a very significant economic opportunity for many local communities.

Tourism and Aid

Multilateral and bilateral aid agencies are wary of involving themselves in the tourism sector. In 1969 the World Bank created a Tourism Projects Department recognising that in the Mediterranean and Adriatic countries, and in Mexico, tourism had been a significant generator of foreign exchange and of direct and indirect employment, internationally in the late nineteen sixties, there was considerable concern about high rates of unemployment and the ability of developing countries to service debt. Tourism sector studies were completed in some 31 countries and tourism staff regularly participated in World Bank macro-economic missions—their reports focussed on the potential for growth in tax revenues, foreign exchange earnings and, direct and indirect employment effects. The primary emphasis was on national economic impact. By 1978 when the World Bank closed its Tourism Projects Department of the Bank had provided loans and credits for 18 projects in 14 countries and it was the major source of funds and technical assistance for tourism development. The Bank withdrew from tourism development for a range of reasons amongst which were anxieties about the role of the Bank in funding projects to develop luxury hotels designed to attract wealthy travellers from the developed countries. This strategy was seen inconsistent with new policy objectives which prioritised the bottom 40 per cent, the Bank's priorities were shifting towards the poor, a group which was gaining relatively little from tourism development. There was a growing literature that focussed on the negative economic, social and cultural impacts of unmanaged tourism on local communities. The fuel crises of the nineteen seventies also undermined some of the forecasts that had been made for the strength of the market and the Bank withdrew from the sector in parallel with most other multilateral and bilateral agencies.

The international agencies followed a macro-economic tourism agenda in the nineteen seventies and eighties focusing on tax and foreign exchange revenues at the national level, major hotel and resort development, international promotion and national and regional master planning all attracted funding. In the nineties the adoption of the new poverty elimination target of halving the number of people living on less than one US $ per day by 2015 refocussed development assistance on pro-poor growth. Multilateral and bilateral aid agency agendas are shifting towards micro-economic growth strategies, which benefit local communities and in particular those below the poverty threshold. With poverty elimination now at the heart of decision aid, the potential for using tourism to generate pro-poor economic growth is being reassessed.

Since the mid-1980s, interest in 'green' tourism, eco-tourism and community tourism has grown rapidly among tour operators, policy-makers, advocates and researchers. All of these focus on the need to ensure that tourism does not erode the environmental and cultural base on which it depends. The emphasis has been on minimising social, cultural and environmental impacts; rather than on positively affecting the livelihoods of the poor.

The Potential of Pro-Poor Tourism

There are a number of reasons to look again at tourism and to assess its potential to generate pro-poor growth. Eighty per cent of the world's poor live in just 12 countries and tourism is significant or growing in all but one of them. Tourism is a very large sector, it is growing rapidly, and there is some evidence that it is relatively labour-intensive. The consumer travels to the destination, creating additional—local—opportunities for the sale of additional goods and services—ranging from local pottery to a guided walk. Tourism can be used to diversify local economies; it can often be developed in remote and marginal areas with few other diversifications or export opportunities. These areas often attract tourists because of their high landscape, cultural and wildlife values. These natural resources and the local culture are amongst the few assets of the poor.

Pro-poor tourism generates net benefits for the poor. It can be defined as forms of tourism where the benefits to the poor are greater than costs which tourism brings them. Economic costs and benefits are clearly important but social environmental and cultural costs and benefits are also need to be taken into account. Pro-poor tourism aims to expand opportunities for those living on less than one US $ per day. Whilst it will also need to be sustainable preserving local culture, minimizing environmental impacts, it will be driven by the poverty agenda. Community-based tourism seeks to promote initiatives by local communities or individuals within them; much has been learnt from these projects. Maximizing the poverty elimination effect requires that the emphasis is placed on involving those people who are living on less than one US $ per day and creating economic opportunities for them. Not all community tourism is pro-poor in this sense.

Effects on the Livelihoods of the Poor

Assessing the livelihood impacts of tourism is not simply a matter of counting jobs or wage income. Participatory poverty assessments demonstrate great variety in the priorities of the poor and factors affecting livelihood security and sustainability. Tourism can affect many of these, positively and negatively, often indirectly. It is important to assess these impacts and their distribution.

Tourism can generate four different types of local cash income generally involving different categories of people:

- Wages from formal employment;
- Earnings from selling goods, services, or casual labour (e.g., food, crafts, building materials, guide services);
- And profits arising from locally owned enterprises
- Income: This may include profits from a community run enterprise, dividends from a private sector partnership and land rental paid by an investor.

Waged employment can be sufficient to lift a household from insecure to secure. But it may only be an available to a minority, and not to the poor. Casual earnings per person may be very small, but much more widely spread and may be enough, for instance, to cover school fees for one or more children. Work as a tourist guide although casual, is often of high status and relatively well paid. There are relatively few examples of successful and sustainable collective income from tourism.

Negative economic impacts include inflation, dominance by outsiders in land markets and in-migration, which erodes economic opportunities for the local poor. Impacts differ between men and women. Women can be the first to suffer from loss of natural resources (e.g., access to fuel wood) and cultural/sexual exploitation, but may benefit most from physical infrastructure improvements (e.g. piped water or a grinding mill) where this is a byproduct of tourism.

Positive Development Impacts of Tourism

On the positive side, tourism can generate funds for investments in health, education and other assets, provide infrastructure, stimulate development of social capital, strengthen sustainable management of natural resources, and create a demand for improved assets (especially education). On the negative side, tourism can reduce local access to natural resources draw heavily upon local infrastructure, and disrupt social networks.

Tourism affects the livelihoods of the poor by changing their access to assets. In several cases, tourism's impact on people's access to natural resources or physical infrastructure has been identified as the most important benefit or concern.

Cultural Impacts of Tourism Can be Positive or Negative

Local residents often highlight the way tourism affects other livelihood goals—whether positively or negatively—such as cultural pride, a sense of control, good health, and reduced vulnerability. Socio-cultural intrusion by tourists is often cited as a negative impact. Certainly sexual exploitation particularly affects the poorest women, girls and young men. The poor themselves may view other types of cultural change as positive. Tourism can also increase the value attributed to minority cultures by national policy-makers. Overall, the cultural impacts of tourism are hard to disentangle from wider processes of development.

The overall balance of positive and negative livelihood impacts will vary enormously between situations, among people and over time, and particularly in the extent to which local priorities are able to influence the planning process. The application of a 'sustainable' livelihood framework is essential to developing pro-poor approaches. The distribution of livelihood impacts has to be considered. The poor are far from being a homogenous group. The positive and negative impacts of tourism will inevitably be distributed unevenly among poor groups, reflecting different patterns of assets, activities, opportunities and choices. The most substantial benefits, particularly jobs, may be concentrated among few. Net benefits are likely to be smallest, or negative, for the poorest.

Policies to Enhance Pro-Poor Tourism

Despite innumerable case studies of tourism development, there is relatively little assessment of practical experience in strategies to make tourism more pro-poor. Nevertheless, lessons can be drawn from a wealth of small initiatives (many from 'community tourism' or 'observation and development' programmes), supplemented by expanding knowledge on 'pro-poor growth strategies', several policy implications clearly emerge.

1. *Put Poverty Issues on the Tourism Agenda*

A first step is to recognise that enhancing the poverty impacts of tourism is different from commercial, environmental or ethical concerns. PPT can be incorporated as an additional objective, but this requires pro-active and strategic intervention. There may well be trade-offs to make, for example between attracting all-inclusive operators and maximising informal sector opportunities, or between faster growth through outside investment, and slower growth building on local capacity. These trade-offs need to be addressed.

2. *Enhance Economic Opportunities and a Wide Range of Impacts*

Two approaches need to be combined:

- Expand poor people's economic participation by addressing the barriers they face, and maximising a wide range of employment, self-employment and informal sector opportunities;

- Incorporate wider concerns of the poor into decision-making. Reducing competition for natural resources, minimising trade-offs with other livelihood activities, using tourism to create physical infrastructure that benefits the poor and addressing cultural disruption will often be particularly important.

3. *A Multi-level Approach*

Pro-poor interventions can and should be taken at three different levels:

- This is where pro-active practical partnerships can be developed between operators, residents, NGOs and local authorities, to maximise benefits;
- national policy level policy-reform may be needed on a range of tourism issues (planning, licensing, training) and non-tourism issues (land tenure, business incentives, infrastructure, land-use planning);
- International level—to encourage responsible consumer and business behaviour, and to enhance commercial codes of conduct.

4. *Work Through Partnerships, Including Business and Tourists*

National and local governments, private enterprises, industry associations, NGOs, community organisations, consumers, and donors all have a role to play. It is particularly important to engage business, and to ensure that initiatives are commercially realistic and integrated into mainstream operations. Private operators will not be able to devote substantial time and resources to developing pro-poor actions. NGOs and donors can help in reducing the transaction costs of changing commercial practice—for example, facilitating the training, organisations, and communication that would enable businesses to use more local suppliers. Changing the attitudes of tourists (at both international and national levels) is also essential if pro-poor tourism is to be commercially viable and sustainable.

5. *Incorporate Pro-poor Tourism Approaches into Mainstream Tourism*

Pro-poor tourism should not just be pursued in niche markets (such as eco-tourism or community tourism). It is even more important that mass tourism is developed in ways that benefit the poor. It is also important to assess which tourism segments are particularly relevant to the poor. Domestic tourists are likely to be important customers.

6. *Reform Decision-Making Systems*

It is impossible to prescribe exactly how each tourism enterprise should develop in ways that best fit with livelihoods. The most important principle is to enhance the participation of the poor. Three different ways of doing this can be identified:

- Strengthen rights at local level (e.g., tenure over tourism assets), so that local people have market power and make their own decisions over developments.
- Develop more participatory planning.
- Use planning gain and other incentives to encourage private investors to enhance local benefits. These approaches require implementation capacity among governmental and non-governmental institutions within the destination, and require a supportive national policy framework.

It is time to reconsider the role of tourism in contributing to pro-poor development. Tourism should be judged against other possible strategies and where it offers the best opportunities for pro-poor growth, or where it can make a useful contribution by increasing the diversity of opportunities for the poor, tourism it should be considered. However, careful and effective local management will be essential if it is to contribute to meeting poverty targets and if tourism dependency is to be avoided.

8

Tourism and the Environment

The relationship between tourism and the environment is obvious, and is largely established through what is sometimes called "environment quality". This quality is perceived in different ways according to the human population and the circumstances presiding tourist activities at any given moment. Any analysis of the relationship between tourism and the environment that we can include under human ecology therefore comprises aspects of the natural sciences as well as the social sciences.

Tourist activity is promoted, conditioned and influenced by the environmental circumstances of each region and can be affected by modifications or changes in those circumstances. Although a lot of emphasis has been placed on the negative impact or modifications in "environment quality" attributed to tourism, it is also accepted that it can be a very important factor in the preservation and defence of ecological values threatened by more destructive alternatives for the use of territory. Very often, tourism can be the most suitable and most satisfactory way of using a region's renewable natural resources. Nevertheless, their management and use need to be properly regulated so as to guarantee their renewability and persistence.

There is room in this complex field of relations to study, rationalize and optimize an activity as important as tourism, from the point of view of its insertion in the ecological systems with which it interacts. However, there are relatively few efficient studies on issues of real importance. It is startling to observe that places with tourist potential undertake little or no research in this field.

One possible cause is the difficulty in identifying the real problematic in tourism/environment relations, which is essentially interdisciplinary and involves the integration of traditionally separate areas of knowledge. Although work is undertaken from time to time on environmental psychology, the sociology of tourism, behaviour in relation to the environment, etc., they are very rarely combined with works on the environment, forestry and agricultural policies, soil use, contamination, biodiversity, evaluation of environmental impact, nature conservation, etc., in search for a more integrated management of tourist resources.

Responsible Tourism

Tourism runs the risk of going the way of other phenomena, which first of all experience rapid growth and then suffer a spectacular collapse, what in Economics is often called "boom and bust".

The causes are familiar: a certain dose of greed, often based on a lack of mid- or long-term planning, property speculation, little consideration for local populations—in both economic and social aspects—and, in general, a lack of awareness as regards environmental aspects—contamination, water use, energy, etc., — on the part of tour operators, hoteliers and other agents involved in tourism in its different forms, including the tourists themselves. The problem is particularly evident in ecotourism, based on the wonders of the natural world: landscapes, flora and fauna. Many experts fear for the future of this type of tourism, which has grown spectacularly in the last few years. Landscapes deteriorate, the fauna decreases, the designers and administrators of tourist developments fail to respect the most elementary principles for adapting architecture to its surroundings, or else there is little effort to recycle, economise or educate with a few honourable exceptions, tourist planning is careless and irresponsible.

And yet a responsible approach would be in the tour operators' own interests, as it would make the tourist industry sustainable, with positive influences on biological, economic and social aspects.

Ecotourism, for example, has shown that when properly conceived it can become a powerful instrument for the preservation of nature, with very favourable repercussions for local populations and for educational programmes, while offering hundreds of millions of ecotourists a wide range of spiritual and physical satisfactions. At the same time, the host countries can take pride in what they have to offer their citizens and the rest of the world.

The preventive and corrective measures are known to us; what is needed is a sense of responsibility and farsightedness on the part both of the authorities and of the industry. We need regulations and controls, so as to put the people who do the damage out of circulation and reward those at the forefront of sustainability

Sustainable Tourism

After several decades of rapid quantitative growth, tourism is going through a period of profound transformation. Tourists, the consumers in this industry, but also the public, have started to demand a change in the conditions of production and use of tourist services, putting an end to the uncontrolled expansion of mass tourism.

This is the ultimate reason, apart from ethical and aesthetic considerations, why tourist activity as a whole, in the private sector as well as in the public and voluntary (NGO) sector, has begun to seriously analyse the implications of tourism in terms of socio-cultural and environmental impacts, and to consider the need to draw up and implement environment friendly tourist policies.

Indeed, while not denying the viability and the utility of alternative approaches of an external and coercive nature, it is obvious that the decision-makers in the sector react better to positive stimuli. The realisation that their clients prefer well-conserved areas and non-aggressive tourist practices and that they are prepared to pay more for this makes it easier to adopt strategies of sustainability in the tourist industry in a sincere alliance with conservation movements.

All this points to the validity of Overall Quality Management as a viable method in sustainable tourist activities. The overall quality approach renders the management of products and especially of tourist areas extremely sensitive to the preferences and expectations of consumers. The private public profitability of a tourist destination will depend on client's satisfaction, since these will return more often and for longer and will pass on a positive image of their holiday experiences. In so far as these preferences and expectations include the demand for unspoilt settings, consumer satisfaction, and therefore the profitability of a tourist spot, will call for the development of strategies for sustainable development.

One can believe this is a productive approach for sustainability in the tourist business and one that makes for professional attitudes that fit in with the economic targets of businesses and other organisations. There is only one prior requirement: continued education and training of everyone involved in tourism, from consumers to those responsible for tourist policies. The demand for quality, and even more so for environmental quality, is a call to people's awareness, to their understanding of the environmental and cultural implications of any activity and their ability to express themselves and to organise to choose the most clear-sighted line of action.

Tourism in the Modern Age

What will the tourist trade of the year 2000 be like? Who will be the tourists of the coming millennium? These are the questions which, faced with the extraordinary boom in tourism, experts, tour operators and politicians have repeatedly posed over the last fifteen years. These questions arise either because of the financial profits the tourist industry involves, or from the demands of consumers who show new awarenesses, habits and lifestyles. In the eighties, mass tourism gradually changed and people began to talk of "tourisms". Expressions such as cultural tourism, sports tourism, religious tourism, adventure tourism or ecotourism have become part of everyday language. In the past, the dominant practices was to take one long holiday in a single destination, today, people tend to distribute their holidays over different destinations and different times of the year.

From a socio-historical point of view, three types of tourist industry can be differentiated. In the case of the industrial tourist, for whom work is the center of existence, the motivations for travelling can be summed up as rest and freedom from responsibilities. This type is gradually decreasing in number. The hedonistic tourist belongs to the generation that discovered entertainment and consumerism. They like to go on holiday to experiment, to explore the unknown, enjoy themselves meet other people and relax in unspoilt natural surroundings. These are the majority today and will continue to be so. Finally, the modern age tourist, someone who tends to reduce the polarity between work and play: not just work, but just not fun, either. Their reasons for travelling include broadening their personal horizons and getting back to simple things and nature, with a touch of creativity in the planning of their journey. These are gradually growing in number and in future will form an important segment of demand.

One characteristic in the expectations of the modern age tourist is the capacity to make a critical appraisal of the offer and to influence it. Producers should be more attentive and sensitive to the new demands and be flexible enough to cater for the tourist in search of higher quality. In the third millennium in fact, the concept of quality will have to take environmental aspects more into account. Recent forms of tourism point to a renewed interest in nature and a wish for quality tourism. So much so, that some tourist spots are reorganising their own offer in keeping with these trends. Quality is the result of a complex strategy which is organised day by day. The consumers, whose environmental awareness is constantly growing, will expect to identify, verify and be able to differentiate ecologically correct products from the imitations now invading the market.

The present millennium is coming to an end and is leaving Western countries with a high level of welfare and a large tourist demand to satisfy. Nevertheless, serious environmental problems also plague areas that receive a high influx of tourists. Tourists, tour operators, local authorities and the general public are therefore called on to find new forms of coexistence and the right solutions for themselves and for the survival of the planet.

9

Biodiversity

As human population has surged this century, the populations of numerous other species have tumbled, many to the point of extinction. Indeed, we live amid the greatest extinction of plant and animal life since the dinosaurs disappeared some 65 million years ago, with species losses at 100 to 1,000 times the natural rate. But humans are not just witnesses to a rare historic event, we are actually its cause. The leading sources of today's species loss, habitat alteration, invasions by exotic species, pollution, and overhunting are all a function of human activities.

Human activities have pushed the percentage of mammals, amphibians, land fish that are in "immediate danger" of extinction into double digits. The principal cause of species extinction is habitat loss—the result of encroachment by humans for settlements, for agriculture, or to claim resources such as timber. A particularly productive but vulnerable habitat is found in coastal areas, home to 60 per cent of the world's population. Coastal wetlands nurture two-thirds of all commercially caught fish, for example. And coral reefs have the second highest concentration of biodiversity in the world, after tropical rainforests. But human encroachment and pollution are degrading these areas: roughly half of the world's salt marshes and mangrove swamps have been eliminated or radically altered, and two-thirds of the world's coral reefs have been degraded, 10 per cent of them "beyond recognition". As coastal migration continues—coastal dwellers could account for 75 per cent of world population within 30 years—the pressures on these productive habitats will likely increase".

Habitat loss tends to accelerate with an increase in a country's population density. This is bad news for the world's biodiversity hotspots-species-rich ecosystems at greatest risk of destruction. Twenty-four of these hotspots, containing half of the planet's species, have been identified globally. Some of the most important hotspot countries will reach population densities that have been linked with very high rates of habitat loss. Five of the six most biologically rich countries could see more than two-thirds of their original habitat destroyed by 2050 if this historical relationship holds.

Related to loss of habitat is the growing incidence of plant, animal, insect, and microbial invasions of ecosystems worldwide as human interchange increases. These "exotic species" sometimes dominate local ecosystems, eliminating native species and reducing overall diversity. Exotics are implicated in 68 per cent of all fish extinctions in the United States this century, for example. Growth in human travel and commerce explains many accidental invasions by exotics, but foreign species are also deliberately introduced into farms, plantation forests, and aquaculture systems. Although only one per cent of exotics cause widespread damage, exotic species are the second leading cause, after habitat destruction, of species loss worldwide.

Other, often diffuse effects of expanded human activities also disrupt ecosystems. Nitrogen, for example, is now made available to plants at more than twice the preindustrial rate as a result of fertilizer production, cultivation of nitrogen-fixing crops, and the burning of fossil fuels. This overfertilisation of the Earth favours some species at the expense of others, leading to a reduction in diversity and resiliency of land and aquatic ecosystems.

Likewise, greenhouse gas emissions could disrupt ecosystems on a vast scale. As with nitrogen, increased levels of atmospheric carbon may favour some species over others: annuals over perennials, for example, or deciduous trees over evergreens. To the extent that greenhouse gases induce changes in global climate, many species may be at risk as habitats shift or shrink, and as some life forms, such as insects or animals, adapt and migrate more quickly than others, such as plants. And as sea levels rise with a change in climate, ecosystems such as coastal wetlands could be destroyed.

10

Population Growth and Natural Recreation Areas

Population growth during the past 50 years has made it difficult to set aside and conserve natural areas. Another half-century of growth will put even more pressure on protected areas as formerly small, distant settlements encroach on these sites and as the number of people (both local and visitors) who use these sites explodes.

National parks, forests, wildlife preserves, beaches, and other protected areas offer sanctuary to various habitats and indigenous communities, in addition to providing resources for local peoples. In an urbanizing world, these sites provide an opportunity for healthy interaction with the natural environment, as well as rare serenity.

From Buenos Aires to Bangkok, dramatic population growth in the world's major cities and the sprawl and pollution they bring—threatens natural recreation areas that lay beyond city limits. Tremendous growth in the population of Bombay has already engulfed Borivili National Park, a reserve that was boyond the city's periphery only a decade ago. With projected growth of 60 per cent in the next 20 years, Bombay may soon swallow up more distant areas. On every continent, human encroachment has reduced both the size and the quality of national recreation areas.

In nations where rapid population growth has outstripped the carrying capacity of local resources, protected areas become especially vulnerable. Although in industrial nations these areas are synonymous with camping, hiking, and picnics in the country, in Asia, Africa and Latin America most national parks, forests, and preserves are inhabited or used for natural resources by local populations.

An assessment by the World Conservation Union—IUCN of 30 protected sites in the developing world shows that these areas now act as magnets, attracting people to the rich oasis of water, fuel, food, and other resources they contain. Population growth rates in and around these areas are typically 2 percentage points above the national average—largely as a result of immigration from resource-starved areas.

As people seek out scarce resources, the resulting concentrations can be devastating. For example, population densities in the region surrounding Bwindi Impenetrable National Park in southern Uganda are some of the highest in all of Africa—exceeding 250 people per square kilometer. Though population at this site is expected to multiply, chronic land hunger already precipitates conflicts over fuel-wood collection, farming, cattle grazing, and bush burning.

Migration-driven population growth also endangers natural recreation areas in many industrial nations. Everglades National Park faces collapse as millions of newcomers move into South Florida.

Coastal recreation areas, including beaches, may be most burdened by the formidable combination of population growth and migration. All but one of the world's 15 largest cities—Mexico City—are coastal, and all of these cities will grow in the decades ahead. Whether it takes the form of expanding shanty towns in Kingston, Jamaica, or sprawling tract housing in southern California, virtually all the growth and movement in population in the next 50 years will occur in densely populated coastal corridors.

In nations already struggling to meet basic human needs, the prospect of establishing additional protected areas becomes increasingly slim. Throughout India, for example, while the national government designates areas as protected, state and local governments work to de-reserve these sites so that the resources can be harnessed to meet the needs of an additional 18 million Indians each year.

Sunbathers on beaches in Japan are often compared to sardines. People who use Central Park in New York City, which has nearly doubled in population since 1950, are faced with growing congestion and restrictions on activities. National parks throughout North America are confronted with huge backlogs of requests to visit, having to turn tourists away. Tourism at Yosemite has boomed from roughly 4,000 visitors in 1886 to more than 4 million people (and their cars) today. It is often remarked that "Americans love their national parks to death", as increased visitation degrades campsites, trails, and wilderness.

Longer waiting lists and higher user fees for fewer secluded spots are likely the tip of the iceberg, as population growth threatens to eliminate the diversity of habitats and cultures, in addition to the space and quiet, that protected areas currently house.

11

Economics and Sustainable Development

Economists and ecologists were once seen as enemies: environmental protection, it was thought, could only be achieved at the expense of economic growth. The misconception persists at the extremes among both the most fundamentalist Greens and the most ideological free marketers. But increasingly it is now being recognised that development and care for the environment go hand in hand. This interdependence is coalescing in the new and necessary discipline of environmental economics.

Conventional economics patterns have often assumed that growth and technical progress will nullify all resource and environmental limits. Environmental economics recognises that the world's natural capital underpins all development, and that it is rapidly becoming scarcer as human demands exceed the globe's long-term carrying capacity. Government of India has introduced environmental measures over the last two decades, but need to move further towards integrating them into economic policies. There can be no real sustainable development unless environment and development policies are integrated at the very beginning of the decision-making process.

Quantifying the Environmental Cost

One of the first steps is to work out the true costs of polluting and depleting the World's natural resources, such as its soil, air and water, the climate and the ozone layer. There have often been regarded as free goods, and it was believed that the world has an infinite capacity to absorb the effects of human activities. Environmental economists, recognising that the social and economic costs of degradation are very great, are trying to quantify them. They say that this will make possible better use of such tools as cost-benefit analysis, environmental impact assessment and risk assessment—and the production of national income accounts which reflect the depletion an degradation of natural resources. As these costs are identified and quantified, economic policy can increasingly be developed with sustainable development as the primary objective. Achieving sustainable development requires industrialized and developing countries to make dramatic changes in national and international policies based on a global partnership. The greenhouse effect, the destruction of the ozone layer, the extinction of species and contamination of the oceans, and other environmental problems, affect us all, no matter which corner of the globe we inhabit.

The first and essential step in overcoming a difficulty is to recognize it and understand it. Concern over the difficulties related to sustainability has led scientists and national and international institutions to study the concept and suggest ways of meeting its many requirements. Indicators have been established to measure pollution levels, soil erosion, salinisation, deforestation and a host of environmental problems. Evaluating the impact of such natural resource-use on ecosystems is a major step towards finding the necessary solutions

For example, it has become clear, on a macro-economic level, that national accounting systems fail to reflect these effects adequately, Deterioration of the world's rivers, land degradation, air pollution and contamination of the seas are not taken into consideration. Inadequate accounting distorts reality and gives a false idea of the true consequences of growth and production.

On a micro-economic level, much is being done to redefine production costs. Incorporating the cost of waste management and internalizing negative external impacts within production prices are beneficial aspects of the economics of sustainability.

Steps are being taken to evaluate public and commonly held assets and to put a price on them, even though they may not be subject to market forces. These are only in the earliest stage but they will allow for more accurate evaluation of the world's natural capital. Fiscal, market, quota and other instruments are being developed to enforce change in the way in which certain resources are used. Examples include markets for transferable emission quotas or compensatory taxation mechanisms designed to ensure that economic forces act to reduce greenhouse gas emissions. Efforts at impact analysis—and in a general sense, cost-benefit analysis—permit rough estimations of the impact that projects might have no ecosystems.

Long-term Repercussions

These instruments carry significant limitations but they are important nevertheless because they attempt to quantify impacts on the natural world and to achieve a more rational use of natural resources. The development of such instruments and evaluation techniques will have significant repercussions in the formulation of sustainable long-term policies. But we must bear in mind that sustainability is not just an economic issue: it is also a political and cultural one.

The concept of sustainability demands as alternative view point in which humankind and the natural world are perceived as a unit—as different yet mutually sustaining aspects of a whole. This perception is not incompatible with progress. It does not renounce development. It simply seeks to affirm life and refuses to discriminate between the means and the end.

It understands that happiness cannot be achieved by destructive means. The questions of how to produce and how to consume therefore become extremely important. Neither should be at the expense of the future or of the natural world. Efficiency is not limited to the links between investment, products and prices: it must address the rational use of resources, including environmental and cultural consequences, both in the long- and the short-term.

Very considerable adjustments must be made in the interests of sustainable development. They demand a reassessment of all our activities which cannot, logically, be done overnight. It is a long and continuous process, characterized by steadfastness and compromise.

12

Living with Diversity

Fishers' nets and loggers' saws may directly impoverish local ecosystems, but most biological losses have root causes far away, in long-settled urban areas and farms where diversity is seldom a concern, but where steadily rising demand for food, water, wood and other resource—and the dispersal of resulting wastes—reach far beyond the settled areas themselves. In general, these peopled landscapes have lost much of their own biological wealth, but what remains is still important to their continued functioning and livability. Reconciling farms and cities with diversity will require stopping the damage they bring to remaining natural habitats, but also beginning to halt and reverse the homogenisation of these unnatural habitats.

Uniformity is not inherently undesirable. In fact, to some degree, homogeneity is the basis of all agriculture: a given type of plant is favored and others are suppressed or eliminated. But trends in recent decades (most notably the Green Revolution and the parallel intensification of farming systems in industrial nations) have pushed uniformity to dangerous levels.

The unsustainability of modern agriculture is in part a measure of its inability to tolerate diversity. Both genetic and ecological uniformity—the sameness of fields sown horizon to horizon without interruption—demand costly and often futile reliance on chemicals to protect crops from pests or diseases that are rapidly spreading and evolving.

The drive to leave no hectare unploughed worsens soil erosion, pushing tractors onto highly erodible hillsides and removing windbreaks, hedgerows and other remnant habitats.

Some of agriculture's biological impacts are obvious—the expansion of farms onto forests and wetlands, for example. While the increasing reliance on chemical inputs and machinery has reduced these impacts in some cases by decreasing the area needed to produce a given amount of food, it has worsened others.

A fundamental transition away from today's wasteful and polluting farming systems is needed to put the world's food supplies on a secure footing. Many of the reforms that will reduce farming's dependence on fossil fuel inputs and its misuse of soils and waters can also restore diversity to agricultural landscapes. Pesticides, for example, kill not only pests but other animals, such as pollinators and predators, that are beneficial to agriculture. Alternative pest control measures that lower pesticide use can also, ironically, reduce pest damage to crops by reviving the diversity of soil and insect communities, which play crucial roles in maintaining soil productivity and checking the spread of pest outbreaks.

Traditional agro-ecosystems are important not only because they provide sustenance to rural people and harbor valuable genetic resources, but also because they contain the seeds of a sustainable, diversity-based mode of agriculture. At varying levels, diversity is the basis of production for many peasants. Farmers often mix strains of a given crop in their fields as a hedge against the vagaries of weather. They also tend to recognize the dependence of their farms on adjacent ecological systems and to tolerate wild plants (often crop relatives whose continued interbreeding with domestic descendants contributes to genetic variety) on the outskirts of their fields.

Population growth and the expansion of large commercial farms have rendered many once-sound practices no longer viable, and traditional agriculture badly needs infusions of money and research to increase its modest yields without abandoning its stability.

Urban areas, with good reason, are considered the antithesis of natural diversity. Only the most resilient creatures (many of them regarded as weeds and pests) thrive in them, and cities' ceaseless expansion, consumption of resources, and emissions of waste threaten both farmland and wilderness almost everywhere. As with agricultural lands, the first priority for urban areas is to half their expansion on to other ecosystems and reduce the damage they export, such as the sewage poured onto coral reefs by burgeoning coastal cities throughout the tropics, or the wasteful consumption of tropical hardwoods in Japanese building construction.

But even concrete jungles can support some diversity. Landscaping of private yards and public spaces with native vegetation can not only reduce the expense and environmental impact of watering, spraying and hauling the remains of sterile grass monocultures, but also help revive bird and other wildlife populations. Most urban areas also have water-ways running through them, or corridors of unused land such as steep ravines; if their use as waste receptacles is reduced, these can be maintained or restored as wildlife habitat.

In developing nations, especially, a surprising amount of agricultural production takes place within city limits, in home gardens. These hidden farmlands contain a great deal of genetic diversity, and their expansion could help reduce the scale and environmental impacts of commercial agriculture.

One reason that the destruction of biological diversity has gone so far without major public commitments to stopping it is that urban dwellers have little experience of the natural and even less understanding of its importance. Restoring nature where people live—reestablishing a personal link with the living world—may be necessary to save it elsewhere. For all the rational arguments favouring long-term protection of biological assets, people who have lost all direct sense of their dependence on natural systems may simply not care.

Only a growing respect for diversity for its own sake—beginning, perhaps, with a reconnection between people and nature within the urban environment—will trigger altruistic responses among those wealthy enough to have the option of considering the needs of future generations and natural communities. Although many conservation measures make economic sense, arguments of economics or self-interest will likely fail to be convincing when the contest is between a few uncharismatic species of unknown value and a major industrial project. "Human beings make sacrifices for what they love." Those who maintain strong bonds with the biological world on which they depend may be more inclined to make the hard decisions needed to protect it.

13

Fresh Water and the Environment

It is widely recognized that water is going to be one of the major issues confronting humanity at the turn of the century and beyond. We are facing a crisis as regards the quantity and quality of water supply, but we have yet to experience full social and political impact of that crisis. The escalation in the population and the quest for continued development is leading to conflicting pressures on water resources. Such resources are the ultimate recipient of pollution from various socio-economic activities associated with urbanisation, agriculture, mining and clearing of native vegetation. Pollution originating from human waste, especially where appropriate sanitation facilities are not available, or are located too close to water supply sources affects both surface water and ground water.

This makes water supply and health perhaps the most important issue for the large proportion of the global population. Paradoxically, the demands for "sustainable management" and increasing global population require more potable water from a declining available potable water base.

It is universally accepted that proper water administration is a critical component of sustainable development—that is, development that meets the needs of both present and future generations. Indeed, water is an essential factor in a large number of productive activities, of which one of the most important is the production of food by irrigation. This activity, accounts for two-thirds of the water resources used by humanity. A supply of drinking water and sanitation in urban centres are crucial for preserving human health.

For some decades it has been known that the misuse of water resources is responsible for many important environment problems. For example, in many industrialized cities both surface water and ground water are seriously contaminated. This deterioration is a consequence of a range of human activities, sometimes in isolation, others over a large area or a long period of time. Among examples of the latter is modern agriculture, whether it uses irrigation or not, as a result of the intensive use made of mineral fertilizers and pesticides.

Water Shortage: Exaggeration, Reality or Bad Management?

Some of these problems have made news and have created the impression the water shortage will be one of humanity's big problems in the coming decades. Sometimes this feeling is due to genuinely manipulative publicity campaigns to justify the setting in motion of hydraulic megaprojects which basically benefit a few large construction companies. The truth is that except for a handful of very specific cases, no problems of water shortage are to be found almost anywhere. On the other hand, cases of bad water management are not rare at all.

Basic Principles for Good Water Management

Good management of water resources—and of almost all other natural resources—must be based on the principles of solidarity, "subsidiarity" and participation. The physical reality requires that these resources be considered a common heritage of humanity both now and in the future. By "subsidiarity" we mean that water management should be as decentralized as possible: what one person or any minor social group can do should not be done by a higher authority. For example, what local government can do should not be done by a regional, state or central government. Participation consists in water users playing as large a part as possible in decisions affecting water, in keeping with each state's or country's social and cultural structure. Obviously this participation calls for a certain cultural and technical knowledge—a hydrological education—on the part of those users.

The need for participation by users is even greater in the exploitation of groundwater. In this case, users tend to extract water independently of one another. They often fail to realize, until there is a serious economic or environmental impact, that their pumping affects other people who rely on the same water supply as has happened.

Water shortage is rarely a serious problem: in fact, in some cases the problem is exaggerated to justify the construction of large works using taxpayer's money. On the other hand, the contamination of surface and groundwater tends to be a problem which rarely receives adequate treatment. Successful water management should be based on three basic principles: solidarity, subsidiarity and participation. The specific way in which these principles are applied will vary from one state or country to another, but the effectiveness of water management will depend in large measure on the hydrological education of the general public.

The universal way of obtaining freshwater is from rain. River systems are the results of the excess water that falls on dry land in the form of rain. On the one hand, rainwater penetrates the permeable soils, saturates them and accumulates to form groundwater reservoirs, or aquifers, which can come to the surface in the form of springs. On the other hand, the water is absorbed by vegetation, which uses it for pumping minerals and then evaporates it by transpiration. Some rainwater is lost because it evaporates immediately on falling on impermeable surfaces like the asphalt of roads and cities. Running water courses finally flow over saturated soils, shaping the complex systems of the watersheds or river basins.

Since each basin's natural system has developed gradually and has grown up according to the yearly distribution and fluctuations of rainfall, we have to appreciate that any large-scale project for redistributing water by means of pipes, as if it were gas or electricity, is a journey into the unknown. This is because it destroys the results of the work of shaping the climate, however transitory it might be.

Variable Volumes

All water supplies are of variable volume. Both the discharge of rivers and the level of lakes and aquifers depend on rainfall. As these resources are components of a large system, the river basin, a reasonable policy would be to manage water resources according to the characteristics of each basin. This would require, first of all, a proper understanding of the system so as to adapt use and consumption to the existing supply. Conserving river systems as much as possible in their natural state is the best guarantee for the preservation of the landscape and of a constant supply. Grondwater reservoirs aren't canals, but are more like lakes, so that pollution leads to the build-up of a debt which is paid in years to come.

Consumption

Water consumption has increased in recent years as a result of not only population growth but also an increase in living standards. In the rural areas the introduction of new farming methods, the spread of irrigation and the excessive use of fertilizers and pesticides causes very high consumption—it is estimated that more than 2/3 of water consumption is used in irrigation. Agricultural pollution also endangers both surface water and aquifers, which receive water full of chemical products. Many cases of eutrophication, the enrichment of water by nutrients that accelerate the growth of algae, derive from the run-off of fertilizers. The practice of intensive stock-raising on farms with large numbers of animals also brings about these problems of over-consumption and pollution. Cleaning the stockyards requires large amounts of water which is then released into the environment with high concentrations of nitrogen.

As for industries, they have in the past taken little care over water consumption and dumping, and in many areas the need for proper attention comes as something new. The best thing would be to make industry take its water at a point down-river from where it returns or, better still, generalise the use of closed circuit systems based on the constant recycling and reusing of the same water.

As regards human consumption, the general attitude to cleanliness is based on diluting pollutants. One example is the success of the use of the Water Closet which involves diluting a few decilitre of urine in 10 or more litres of drinking water: quite a record in wastefulness.

Another aspect to be considered is the different quality of the water that falls on well formed soils from the water that falls on roads, cities, airports, suburbs and built-up areas and whose composition is less stable and "worse" than that resulting from a more uniform interaction with mature soils. Remember that streets, roofs, communication routes, airports and built-up areas already cover a high proportion of the earth's land area and are still on the increase.

Purification techniques should be based especially on the natural processes that include biological activity. Otherwise—for example, if physico-chemical methods are used—there can be side-effects such as an excess of mud or sediments. The strategy to follow is to optimize operations in our use of water according to the discharge and to the distribution of contamination. A system in the form of a conduit or channel, such as a river, can respond relatively quickly. On the other hand, lakes and dams can only do so up to a point, because they show more inertia and irreversibility and take longer to clean.

Large lakes, not to mention the sea, might seem a good place to dump contaminating refuse, but they can't then be cleaned. This is the price we pass on to the future generations: a comfortable attitude, but an unacceptable one.

14

Ecosystems, Our Unknown Protectors

How ecosystems work and what part they play in biodiversity remain a mystery, but we do know that they perform a host of invaluable services for the human species. In my view, biodiversity's fundamental value is neither aesthetic nor economic but environmental, even though most people are largely unaware of this. The value of biodiversity is often measured in terms of the number of species living in a given area. But the interactions between the many species in an ecosystem, and between them and the environment's physical and chemical components are also very important. This highly intricate web of relationships makes an ecosystem more valuable than the sum of the species it contains.

Ecosystems perform services that are essential for the survival of the human species. They fix carbon in the atmosphere and produce oxygen, protect soil from erosion and keep it fertile, filter water and replenish aquifers, provide pollination and anti-parasite agents and so on.

The first two of these services are closely related to each other. They result from photosynthesis, whereby green plants, starting with algae, absorb carbon-di-oxide (CO_2) and emit oxygen. For millions for years, the balance between the various gases in the atmosphere remained stable. But with the coming of the industrial revolution, humans began burning increased amounts of fossil fuels. Today, three billion tonnes of carbon build up in the atmosphere each year, and natural ecosystems can no longer absorb all these emissions—especially since they are disappearing at an alarming rate. Deforestation alone releases such tremendous amounts of CO_2 and other gases, such as methane, that it has become the second-leading cause of global warming.

Storing fresh water, protecting soil and keeping it fertile are three other closely related functions. Ecosystems are veritable "freshwater factories". They absorb rainwater and slowly filter it through the soil before draining it towards streams, rivers, lakes and underground aquifers that supply us with the precious liquid. When the vegetal ground cover is degraded, the water cycle is disrupted. Rain strikes the bare earth, washing away huge amounts of nutritional substances. Reservoirs, lakes and rivers silt up.

Uncertain Reaction to Climate Change

Despite years of research, scientists still know very little about how ecosystems work. We are generally incapable of predicting how they will react to certain transformations in the environment, especially climate changes. Nor do we know any more about whether a species present in a given environment is superfluous or "replicable", even when it is very rare. Likewise, we do not know which key species are indispensable to maintaining an ecosystem, with a few exceptions such as pine forests, where that tree is obviously the dominant species.

We know even less about the part biological diversity itself play in maintaining ecosystems and the services they perform. One simple example is a highest diversified forest that absorbs carbon-di-oxide—a vital function, as we have seen, for limiting global warming. Suppose the forest is cleared to make way for a single-crop forest. The service will still be performed, perhaps even better at first because young, fast-growing trees absorb more CO_2 than old ones, which regenerate slowly. But what will happen in the long term? After several decades, the consequences of the loss of biodiversity will probably be felt. Replacing many species with a single one will have certainly depleted the soil and, in the long term, slowed down the forest's growth and consequently its ability to absorb CO_2.

More generally, diversified ecosystems seem more productive. Specialists remain wary about their conclusions, but today they believe that biodiversity helps ecosystems to resist alien species and diseases and to recover faster in the event of disruption. In the face of doubt, and to find out more about them, it is better to preserve as many different ecosystems as possible.

A Costly Lesson for New York City

Most people take it for granted that ecosystems will carry on performing services without receiving anything in return. They think nature will continue benefiting humanity, no matter how much damage is done. The survival of organisms other than our own species is perceived as a frill that future generations can live without.

These preconceived ideas are wrong and dangerous as the city of New York has recently come to realize. The city's water has always enjoyed such a good reputation that it was sold throughout the northeastern United States. Its equality was due to Catskill Mountains' natural purification system. But that ecosystem has suffered so much from pollution, especially fertilizer run-off from farms, that by the late 1990s New York's water had become undrinkable. The city planned to build a purification plant, whose cost was put at between six and eight billion dollars, not including the $300 million in yearly operating costs—an astronomical bill for a service that had always been free! The price was so staggering that the city eventually decided to restore the Catskill Mountains' degraded environment at a cost of only one billion dollars.

This story clearly illustrates where our interests lie. We must preserve ecosystems and the conditions that enable our planet to ensure the survival of *Homo sapiens* or, at least, the short-term maintenance of our current quality of life.

15

Forests

Global losses of forest area have marched in step with population growth for much of human history. The two trends rose slowly for millennia, turned upward in recent centuries, and accelerated sharply after 1900. Indeed, 75 per cent of the historical growth in global population and an estimated 75 per cent of the loss in global forested area have occurred in the twentieth century. The correlation makes sense, given the additional need for farmland, pastureland, and forest products as human numbers expand. But since 1950, the advent of mass consumption of forest products has quickened the pace of deforestation.

In some cases, population pressure is still closely linked with deforestation. In Latin America, for example, ranching is the single largest cause of deforestation. Because most meat produced in Latin America is consumed there, and because meat consumption per person has been largely unchanged for several decades, it is likely that expanding population is the principal reason for ranching-related deforestation. In addition, analysts at the World Resources Institute estimate that overgrazing and overcollection of firewood—which are often a function of a growing population—are degrading some 14 per cent of the world's threatened frontier forests (large areas of virgin forests). In fact, a U.N. Food and Agriculture Organisation study showed a one-to-one correlation between population growth and fuelwood consumption in 16 Asian countries between 1961 and 1994.

On the other hand, deforestation created by the demand for forest products tracks more closely with rising per capita consumption in recent decades. Global use of paper and paperboard per person, for example, has doubled (or nearly tripled) since 1961, and most of the increase has come in wealthy countries with low or even stable levels of population growth. Europe, Japan, and North America, with 16 per cent of global population, consume 63 per cent of the world's paper and paperboard and nearly half its industrial wood.

Although consumption and population growth have operated somewhat independently in the late twentieth century, the two forces could coincide in the developing world in coming decades, with substantial consequences for forests. Developing country paper consumption is less than one-tenth the level found in industrialised nations, suggesting that large increases in consumption are likely as these nations prosper. (It also suggests that greater economy is needed in industrial countries). With 80 per cent of the world's people, and as home to all the increase in population in coming decades, even modest growth in per capita paper and wood consumption in developing countries could place substantial pressure on forests. If paper were used by the entire world in 2050 at today's industrial-nation rates, paper production would need to jump more than eight-fold over 1996 level.

This projected growth is unsustainable, given that global use of forest products is already near or beyond the limits of sustainable use. Using data on sustainable forest yields, and assuming that virgin forests are left intact, researchers at Friends of the Earth UK have determined that production of forest products for the world is 25 per cent beyond the most restrictive estimates for sustainable consumption. (Many forests, of course, are already logged well beyond sustainable levels). The most optimistic assessment would allow for a further 35 per cent growth in consumption. Even that spells trouble, however, given a projected global population increase of some 54 per cent over the next half-century, and given the likely increase in consumption from rising prosperity. Lower consumption of forest products and increased recycling in industrial countries can make room for a more prosperous developing world to enjoy the products of the world's forests, but the task will be made easier if population growth everywhere is stabilized sooner rather than later.

If population and consumption eat into the world's forests, the resulting loss of forest services reduces, in turn, a country's capacity to support its population. Forests provide habitat to a diverse selection of wildlife; tropical forests, for example, are home to more than 50 per cent of the world's species. And as storehouses of carbon, forests are key to regulating climate. Deforestation leads to huge releases of carbon: an estimated one quarter of the world's carbon emissions come from forest clearing. Loss of these macro-services undermines the stability and resiliency of the global environment on which economies—and populations—depend. In addition, forests provide services vital to a local population, such as control of erosion, steady provision of water across rainy and dry seasons, and regulation of rainfall. Taken together, the loss of these services due to deforestation can upset local economies and subject local populations to economic instability.

16

Forests

The Earth's Lungs

The world's forest cover is shrinking. Over the past 50 years nearly half of the world's original forest cover has been lost—some 3 billion hectares. Each year another 16 million hectares of virgin forest are cut, bulldozed, or burned.

Between 1980 and 1995 the world lost some 180 million hectares of forest—an area equal the size of Indonesia. While developed countries had a net increase of 20 million hectares due to reforestation, this gain was more than offset by a net decrease of 200 million hectares in the developing world.

Forest have many functions of value both to humanity and to nature itself. Take away the trees, and the intricately linked ecosystem unravels. Forests absorb carbon-di-oxide and produce oxygen, anchor soils, regulate the water cycle, protect against erosion, and provide a habitat for millions of species.

Forests products are essential to the world economy, worth about US $400 billion annually in timber, pulp, paper, and fuel wood. Forest products other than wood, such as medicines, vegetables, and fruits, provide another US $20 billion and are growing in importance.

Healthy forests boost food production. Trees soak up and store water from season to season, slowly releasing moisture during dry periods. Without tree cover, water runs off faster during the tropical rainy season, carrying away valuable topsoil. A World Bank study found that the rate of soil loss was 10 times higher on forest lands where slash-and-burn shifting cultivation was practiced than in undisturbed forests. One reason that agricultural yields have fallen in sub-Saharan Africa is that vast amounts of forests cover have disappeared, hastening soil erosion and loss of soil nutrients.

Forest cover regulates climate, while destruction of forests contribute to global warming. Whereas living trees soak up and store carbon-di-oxide from the atmosphere trees that are cut down and burned release carbon into the atmosphere. In the last decade tropical deforestation has released large amounts of stored carbon—accounting for roughly one-quarter of the carbon-di-oxide emissions to the atmosphere due to human activity.

Pressures on Forests

Current demand for forests products may exceed the limits of sustainable consumption by 25 per cent. The developed world accounts for most of the demand for forest products. With just 16 per cent of the world's population, North America, Europe, and Japan consume two-thirds of the world's paper and paperboard and half its industrial wood. Demand for industrial wood products also has risen in developing countries, however, along with demand for fuel wood, the main energy source for many rural communities.

Throughout the 1990s many developing countries with rapid population growth had high rates of deforestation. Forest land was converted to agricultural use, and trees cut to provide housing and wood for fuel. Moreover developing countries steeped up exports of forests, products to meet the rising demand from developed countries.

The amount of forest area per capita fell by half between 1960 and 1995—reflecting both population growth and the disappearance of forest cover. In 1995 close to 1.7 billion people lived in countries with less than one-tenth of a hectare of forest cover per capita (83). By 2025, an estimated 4.6 billion people will live in such countries.

What Can Be Done?

As population grows and per capita consumption of forest products increases, countries must do more to manage forest resources on a sustainable basis. The following developments offer encouragement.

Technological Improvements

Technological improvements including use of recycled paper and paperboard, have substantially reduced the amount of pulp needed to produce paper. In 1970 paper and paperboard consisted of 80 per cent wood pulp. By 1997 more efficient production processes had reduced that figure to 56 per cent. As a direct result, the production of pulp for paper is expected to grow by just over 1 per cent a year over the next decade, about half the growth rate in the 1980s.

Forest Products Certification

Adopting a system that identifies forest products that come from sustainable managed forests could support efforts toward sustainability. As of 1998, about 10 million hectares of forest land has been certified. Over 90 per cent of the certified area is in northern, temperate forests, mostly in Europe and North America. Close to 60 per cent of the entire certified area is in just two countries—Sweden and Poland—reflecting education and awareness campaigns in those countries. In tropical forests, where most of the destruction is taking place today, only tiny areas have been certified as providing sustainable yield.

Inter-governmental Responses

In 1995 the Inter-governmental Panel on Forests (IPF) was established in response to the 1992 Earth Summit. The IPF evolved into the Inter-governmental Forum on Forests in 1997, after the UN's five-year review of the Earth Summit goals. The mission of the forum is to examine the underlying causes of deforestation and to help countries develop strategies that address them.

Efforts to advance an international legal convention on forests, which began in 1990, have been shelved, however. Some observers believe that advancing such a convention would only codify the standards of a weak consensus and thus would be worse than no convention at all. Widespread opposition to a convention makes it unlikely that the issues will reach the negotiating table.

Instead, many organisations urge governments of countries with large forest resources to enforce existing legislation and to introduce more effective forest conservation initiatives close to 130 countries have developed or updated their National Forest Programmes over the past decade.

While such initiatives are promising, they cannot be expected to halt forest destruction completely. Millions of people rely on forest products for their livelihoods. Sustainable forest management will require not just enforcement of laws that project forests but also alternative sources of livelihood for many rural people.

17

International Trade with the Consumer's Money

When trade policies are discussed nationally or internationally people as consumers are largely forgotten. Despite their numbers, they do not carry the weight that producers and other lobbies command. Individually, consumers are seldom informed about how the availability, quality, price and choice of the hundreds of items which they buy in the shops each year are affected by trade policy decisions. If they know how much of their household budgets are determined by decisions to protect individual industries and for how little effect they might be shocked.

Equally, when it is debated publicly, the benefits that would fall to the consumer are usually ignored. This brief study is an attempt to put the consumer interest squarely in the public arena.

How Do Government Decisions on Trade Affect the Consumer?

Virtually all-protective policies mean higher prices for the consumer. And if it is not a consumer who pays, it will be domestic producer. These are some of the main actions taken by national authorities.

Governments frequently and for the most part, legally raise revenue and protect domestic industries by imposing duties on imported products. If a product has a 25 per cent tariff, the price in the shop will normally be 25 per cent more than its price at the port or airport.

Global quotas and other numerical limits on imports are sometimes legal sometimes not. Either way the intention is to restrict access to the market in such a way that domestic producers of the same product can raise their prices without being forced out of business through lack of competitiveness. Quotas are frequently preferred by those demanding protection because the impact on prices is less obvious than with a tariff. Once again, prices go up in the shops and limits may be so narrow that goods disappear from the shelves altogether.

Voluntary export restraints are quotas of an even more costly kind for the importing country. They allow foreign suppliers to charge higher prices than would be possible under a tariff or normal quota. By "bribing" the exporter this way, opposition to the protection is reduced.

Subsidies are sometimes paid to domestic producers to help them compete with import competition by keeping their costs artificially low. This keeps prices down. Unfortunately, the consumer as a tax payer ends up paying for the subsidy. In so doing, he is prevented from keeping more of his income to spend on other goods, which may be produced by more efficient industries. One thing is sure once industries get used to subsidies, it is very hard to wean them away.

Rules permit governments to impose extra duties on imports where products are shown to be dumped (sold below the normal price by the exporting country) or subsidised, and where the effect of dumping or subsidisation is demonstrated to damage the corresponding domestic industry. While these duties may be justified, they nevertheless always serve to raise the price for consumers to knock products completely out of the market. Yet very few, if any, countries give much weight to consumer interest when deciding whether to impose such penalty duties. And their use had grown disturbingly in recent years.

Governments usually impose standards of safety, quality, public health and environmental protection for good reasons often in the interests of consumers. Sometimes, however, the standards and the procedures which enforce them are no more than hidden protection for domestic producers. In imposing unnecessary measures on imports, governments penalize consumers through higher prices and the non-availability of goods.

Protection tends to be loaded towards the products which are essentials for any family. Consequently, since the essentials command the biggest proportion of the household budgets of poor families, protection acts as a regressive tax.

Clothing is a good example. The multifibre arrangement acts on low-cost products, raising prices and restricting availa-bility, meanwhile up-market goods are seldom affected. Moreover, for the poor consumer, the effect is further exaggerated. Foreign producers will tend to export higher quality end, therefore, more expensive goods, in order to maximize their profits from the quota. This quality upgrading effect not only reduces disproportionately the supply of lower-priced clothing, but may also affect the supply of children's clothing.

Consumers have enjoyed an enormous growth in the range and quality of products in their shops as a result of the multi-lateral training system. Many fruit and vegetables are available even out of season throughout the year. Exotic foods, never seen just ten or twenty years ago, are now commonly found on super-market selves. Cut flowers are being transported fresh by cargo plane daily from one country to the other. The range and sophistication of domestic electronic products would have been unimaginable had their development not been spurred by the availability of a global market.

Household Costs are not the only Consumer Cost which Go Up

Many industries are also consumers of imported goods. Manufacturers can depend on cheaper and better products from overseas in order to maintain their own competitiveness in their domestic market and, especially, in their export markets.

The best example is steel. Many companies require either specialty steel or basic steel products at the lowest possible prices. Unfortunately, because of export restraints, formal quotas, anti-dumping and countervailing duties and high tariffs. Sometimes they cannot even find the precise type or quality of steel they need. They are, therefore, put at a huge competitive disadvantage.

Semi-conductors and other electronic components are also subject to this self-defeating form of protection. Just as the price of steel puts up the price of automobiles, so high tariffs, anti-dumping duties and quotas on electronic components puts up the prices of video recorders, personal computers and other advanced consumer electronic products. Meanwhile foreign competitors continue to buy their semi-conductor inputs at world market prices.

But is one of the Prices a Lowering of Public Health and Safety Standards?

It has been suggested that some measures to ensure safe good for consumers and to prevent the spread of pests of diseases among animals and plants do not amount to unjustified barriers to trade.

The first point is that if there is some justification for them, these measures—even if they restrict trade—are completely permissible. The main objective is to make them transparent, to discourage arbitrary decision-making and discrimination and to minimize any restriction on trade.

The second point is that would encourage governments to establish measures consistent with international standards and guidelines. This is important because it could mean a general raising of standards: in many areas even advanced industrial countries do not meet international standards on food safety.

Third, the governments has to impose more stringent standards than those agreed internationally. The only condition is that a government so doing might, if challenged, be required to show scientific evidence or some kind of risk assessment to support the measure.

It should also be noted that with the reduction of agricul-tural subsidies which encourage unlimited production (those supporting farmers' income directly will still be permitted) consumers should see more products produced by less chemical intensive farming methods in the shops.

18

World Trade—The Next Challenge

On 15 December 1993 the world changed. My be not as dramatically as the moment when the Berlin Wall fell, but then unlike that very necessary demolition job, the success of the Uruguay Round was a work of construction. Like the destruction of the wall, though, its effects will be profound and lasting ones felt far beyond its immediate context. It will be seen as a defining moment in modern history.

The importance of the Round can be seen in terms of boost it gives to job creation; to development; to investment; to economic reform; to the rule of law and in many other ways besides. All of these benefits are real and important. But the true value of the whole is much, much more than the sum of these parts.

Put simply, governments came to the conclusion that the notion of a new world order was not merely attractive but absolutely vital; that the reality of the global market—whatever ambitions some of them may retain for regional Integration—required a level of multilateral cooperation never before attempted.

No Losers in the Round

It has created a revolutionary framework for economic, legal and political cooperation. But now turn to the immediate results of the Round. Seeing them as a profit and loss account or a scorecard of winners and losers is to see them in static terms, as one-off conclusions with finite effects. This misses the point completely.

Every nation now needs an effective trading system, but especially so the small and poor. They have it. Everyone will also gain from the huge package of market access results even if they did not get every concession they were seeking from trading partners—it is the biggest market access deal ever negotiated.

However, the essence of the Uruguay Round's achievements is that they are dynamic. The new agreements, the new rules and structures it sets up—all mean a commitment to a continuing process of cooperation and reform of which the agreement in December was only the beginning.

Maintaining the liberalizing momentum will call for continuing effort and vigilance by participating countries. But now their energy can be focused through the Round's greatest innovation; the new World Trade Organisation (WTO) in place of the improvised basis on which the GATT has operated for 45 years, trade will now have a permanent forum appropriate to its importance in the world economy.

Technically speaking, the WTO will oversee the implementation of the Round's results, administer all the agreements in goods, services and intellectual property, and manage the unified dispute settlement system. But beyond these administrative functions, it will raise the political profile of trade which has already been lifted greatly by the Uruguay Round. The WTO will have regular instead of occasional—direct Ministerial involvement. It will have a clear mandate to act as a forum for further trade negotiations. Most of all it will complete the transition from a trading system which largely restricted itself to policies at the border to one which also covers most aspects of domestic policy-making affecting international competition in goods and services, as well as investment.

Through the WTO, the Round will change the way the world economy is shaped. But it is not the final victory over protectionism and unilateralism. Any premature rejoicing would have quickly been cut short by the evidence since 15

December that major economic powers are still ready to take the unilateral approach to trade problems. Arguments for protectionism based on the alleged threat of low-cost competition to production and jobs will not just fade away because the Round is a success. The seductive appeal of "beggar-thy-neighbour" policies is highlighted by the seemingly greater vigour of the lobbies for protectionism than the advocates of open markets.

These dangers—and the speed with which they have resurfaced—make the achievement of the Uruguay Round all the more important, and its successful implementation all the more urgent. Implementation requires more than mutual backslapping about what we have achieved. It requires now that the US, EU and Japan, in particular, rapidly obtain final authority to ratify and also take a lead in providing the WTO with the means to fulfill its mandate.

The success of the Round has come at a time when it is even more vitally needed than anyone could have guessed when it was launched in 1986. Old structures and alignments have been turned inside out in trade as in every other area of international relations. We face a world of change and challenge, in which the reinforced trading system will be a primary source of stability and security.

The developing countries including India have become enthusiastic supporters of the multilateral trading system and the Uruguay Round even if all their demands were not met by industrial countries. The reasons lie in the changing economic policies of many developing countries and the clearer appreciation of the value of the GATT system that has grown along with these changes.

The challenge of new issues in world trade will be a major one for the WTO. The new organisation has to consider issues such as the links between trade and the environment, international competition policy, trade and investment, and trade and labour standards. To say a few words about trade and the environment since it is one area in which GATT member countries have committed themselves already to a comprehensive new work programme. They decided on 15 December, in conjunction with the adoption of the results of the Uruguay Round negotiations, to draw up a work programme on trade and environment by the Ministerial meeting in Marrakesh. Environmental policy-making is one of the most rapidly evolving areas of national and international policy-making, and it is entirely appropriate that emphasis should be placed now in GATT/WTO on ensuring better policy coordination and multilateral cooperation over the linkages between trade and environment.

Permanent Negotiations

The Uruguay Round may well be the last of its kind, but this in no way means the end of multilateral trade negotiations. On the contrary, it means they become a permanent event. Ad hoc negotiating rounds were necessary mainly because the GATT lacked the mandate or the institutional basis to operate the multilateral system to the full on a continuous basis. Between rounds the GATT has tended to lose momentum, often at the very times when it was essential to make the most of the liberalising impulse. This has allowed protectionism and unilateralism to recover and regroup and meant that each round has to start by regaining lost ground.

The positive results of the Uruguay Round will redefine much more than assumptions about trade. If they are exploited with the same determination, courage and commitment that went into concluding the Round, they should mean nothing less than a new start for sustainable growth and a new system of collective economic security for the world.

But if the trading system is now up to the job of supporting multilateral cooperation on such a wide scale, do the other structures of economic cooperation still meet the bill? The establishment of the WTO will put trade and investment on a par—perhaps rather in advance—of cooperation in monetary and financial areas. The WTO will stand alongside its original Bretton Woods sisters, the IMF and the World Bank. The three institutions must learn to work together even more effectively and closely. For example, rather than each body conducting separate reviews of country policies, is there not a case to be made for a more integrated approach on country reviews? But that does not, on its own, add up to effective multilateral economic cooperation. The question really has to be asked seriously: are the G7, the OECD, the regional groupings adequate to provide that cooperation?

It is the next challenge of international economic leadership—the challenge of translating the common interest in global growth into a practical and effective mechanism for solving our common economic problems together. So, the Ministers meeting in Marrakesh is an historic event which will establish the World Trade Organisation and put in place the new multilateral trading system, they will be making not an end, but a beginning.

19

Free Trade as Peacemaker

The Benefits of an Open World Trading System

Globalisation by free trade according to the principles of the World Trade Organisation (WTO) offers the only realistic opportunity to integrate the world peacefully and in time to prevent a major disaster. The primacy of the economy over politics is the most important vehicle for a successful world domestic policy.

Since Adam Smith, traditional economic theory has on principle been well-disposed towards free trade. Free trade enables better use of the world's economic resources than does national protectionism. Countries can concentrate on their respective strength and draw from their trade partners the goods they need, but do not produce. But there have always been objections against free trade.

The international trade system has always been encumbered by disperate accusations of unfair competition. The fear that foreign competitors use unfair methods, such as dumping, as and is widespread. If one were to believe all the charges of dumping that are made, then international trade would have been completely destroyed long ago. Great restraint should be exercised with respect to allegations of dumping if one is interested in maintaining an interweaving of international economic activities.

The Free Trade Opposition Cloaks Itself in Dumping Charges

The modern form of the struggle against free trade cloaks itself in the accusation of ecological dumping or social dumping. With this difficult subject matter, one should not make sweeping generalisations. These things also are not gone into in detail in what follows.

Environmental protection is an asset that every economy produces at the cost of other assets. The people's preferences for the asset of environmental protection probably varies from country to country. It is also completely legitimate and does not at all distort trade if the environmental provisions—in line with the different national preferences—vary from country to country.

In the rich western European economic region, one should guard against a new form of cultural imperialism. It is not for this part of the world to impose its preferences for environmental assets on other countries, especially Third World countries. Free world trade brings not only economic advantages. Even more important is its contribution to lasting world peace.

In view of world population growth, every standstill in the movement towards a peaceful world society must be seen as a step backwards. We are compelled to run a race between the growing problems and the development of stable institutions to overcome them peacefully at global level. Economic history since the end of the Second World War shows clearly that free trade under the old GATT was of decisive importance for the prosperity of the industrialised nations.

The principle of help for self-help has nowhere been applied so consistently as on the free world market. In reverse, the examples of countries that cut themselves off from the world market show the disastrous consequences of the rigidity of a society which shuns the pressure of international competition.

Revolutionary Success of Open-Market Policies

The West's policy of open markets pursued since 1948 and reinforced since 1989 has led to a dynamism which, in the true meaning of the word, is revolutionary. More than half the world population now lives in countries with annual GDP growth rates of more than 5 per cent. Europe is not among that group, which may be why it also stands somewhat apart in its mentality.

Certainly, there also can be undesirable trends in free trade. There is no ideal systems; one must choose between imperfect potentialities. However, no realistically better substitute for the free trade system is in sight, not even with respect to the goals of a pacified world: an ecological sound world economy and a balance of global dimensions between the poor and the rich. An ideal government of philosopher kings armed with absolute power certainly could do something better than does free trade—but such a government remains fictitious. There are tangible and narrow limits to what the political system, whether democratic or not, can effect in a positive sense. This is how the structural conservatism of democratic and other political systems impedes the timely assertion of reforms necessary to achieve a world peace society.

The GATT was turned into the World Trade Organisation (WTO) a few years ago. Besides extending the free trade principle to services and additional agricultural sectors, the new agreement foresees above all the full inclusion of the Third World in the system. The agreement commits the industrialised nations to open their markets to developing and threshold countries.

Other important points are the strengthening and tightening of the dispute mediation process. Based on a system of relatively independent ad hoc panels, it permits complaints against WTO member countries for violations of the agreement. Thus, what is arising here is an effective global jurisdiction within the meaning of a peaceful world domestic policy.

Exclusion as Penalty

The decisive sanction mechanism of the WTO—which is not a specialist organisation of the United Nations—is the threat of exclusion. Exclusion would deny the penalised country free access to the markets of WTO members on the basis of most favoured nation status. This is a threat that requires no armed force, but is very effective. No country can still afford to do without the beneficial effects on prosperity that participation in international trade brings.

Thus, with the threat of denial of access to world markets for violating WTO rules, and the guarantee of a more or less fair competition for a country's own products for abiding by them, a non-military sanctions system has come into being. That is substantial progress on the path to a pacified world.

Certainly, this sanction system's sphere of influence is limited for the time being. Essentially, it will be used to assert the game rules of free trade. It offers no legal grounds for pressing other goals, such as on human rights. Attempting to expand it in this direction would for the foreseeable future put the entire system at risk.

In the current debate on globalisation, the question arises of whether the world economic institutions should not be converted in this manner, that politics regains its autonomy, and that the primacy of politics can be restored. The critics of globalisation point to the constraints to adjust which the world economy exercises on national or continental politics. However well this demand for the primacy of politics may be justified in philosophical terms, it virtually comes down to a demand for the ascendancy of the conservative principle.

Danger of a Slowed-Down World Integration

The demand for the primacy of politics is gaining strength from the desire to avoid the pressure to adjust which the dynamics of world events are exerting. It is today a conservative, and in fact a reactionary, longing for the (Utopian) return of the functioning European welfare state of two or three decades ago. If it were asserted, it would mean practically slowing-down world integration. It would run dead against the goal of a world policy based on a desire for peace.

The present primacy of the economy over politics—in terms of the free movement of goods, services and capital—is basically nothing more than the priority of the global principle over the provincial, the national principle. As such, it gives the principle of change pre-eminence over the principle of maintaining the status quo. What gives the primacy of the economy its legitimacy? Probably not the thought that world peace and better be secured by this means. Its legitimation lies in the very indirect economic success that the free trade system delivers. For the reflective observer, the question remains of whether this legitimation is sufficient.

To answer this question, however, and particularly if one pleads for maintaining the ascendancy of the economy, it appears appropriate to outline the consequences that can be expected from further integration of the world economy. As can be seen today in East and Southeast Asia, the growth dynamics of the world economy will lead to a marked rise in the living standards of a large part of the Third World.

Do not Exclude Poor Countries from the Competition

The global consequences of Asia's growth should not have been seen only negatively. While it also may mean, for example, a great burden on the global climate, it leads at the same time to an acceleration of the process of falling birth rates and thus to an earlier stabilisation of the world population. Prosperity for the Third World is so far the only realistic answer to the urgent problem of population growth. And free competition on the world market in the only reliable means of achieving this prosperity in the course of some decades.

Despite ecological sacrifice in the medium term, continuation of Third World growth is the only way to solve the long-term ecological problems. One also should not forget that only those who can eat their fill and have a roof over their heads are prepared to reflect on ecology and discuss it.

As for the rest, the balance between rich and poor is more acceptable when the poor become richer than when the rich become poorer. That applies also at the international level. The market and access to it are peaceful sanctions of the world economic system on the basis of free trade. Those who are hungry and have nothing more to lose are more of a danger to world peace than those who have eaten their fill. The ruse of covering up domestic problems by cross border military aggression will become less attractive to the degree that a country's own economy is integrated in the global economic system. The more countries are economically dependent on each other, the more unlikely it is that they will wage war on each other.

Globalisation by free trade according to the principles of the WTO offers the only realistic opportunity to integrate the world peacefully and in time to prevent a major disaster. The primacy of the economy is the most important vehicle for a successful world domestic policy.

20

Export Subsidies

A Distortion to Free Trade in Agriculture

Export subsidies are generally considered one of the most distorting trade tools used by governments to interfere with commercial markets. Export subsidies allow a government to determine the level and direction of trade solely on the basis of government subsidies, lowering world prices and denying sales for other, more competitive exporters. Not only are export subsidies unfair commercial tools, but, by encouraging surplus production, they encourage adverse environmental practices, waste government budgets, and may delay restructuring and reform of domestic industries. Substantial progress toward eliminating export subsidies will be a critical element of the World Trade Organisation (WTO) negotiations scheduled to begin at the end of this year.

The Situation Today

Under the Uruguay Round Agreement, countries agreed to strictly limit the use of export subsidies. First, products that had not benefited from export subsidies in the past were banned from receiving them in the future. Second, where countries had provided export subsidies in the past, their future use was capped and gradually reduced over 6 to 10 years. (Developed countries were required to cut their spending on export subsidies by 36 per cent over six years while also reducing subsidised export quantities by at least 21 per cent on a commodity-specific basis. Developing countries have until 2005 to cut spending by 24 per cent and subsidised quantities by 14 per cent). Third, countries agreed not to create new schemes that serve as disguised subsidies to get around the product-specific limits. Finally, countries recognised that export credit and food aid programmes were different and exempted them from the new budget and quantity limits, although there was agreement to negotiate disciplines on export credit programmes to ensure that they do not undermine WTO commitments.

Today, the European Union (EU) is the primary export subsidiser—accounting for nearly 85 per cent of the world total. Nearly all other countries agreed in the last round of negotiations not to use or to have only limited recourse to use export subsidies. EU farmers, responding to domestic prices that are often twice the world price, produce more products than can be consumed in Europe, but at such high prices that they can be sold abroad only with generous subsidies. These subsidies force other competitors out of the market and discourage production in countries with comparative advantage.

If the EU's extravagant domestic subsidies are the root cause of export subsidies, they are also putting serious pressure on the whole EU system. The need to impose budgetary discipline on EU farm programmes (annual cost, about $46 billion) is becoming increasingly evident, even in Europe, and the EU's goal of expanding its membership to new countries is putting pressure on it to bring its farm programmes into line with other countries, which will help reduce its need to rely on export subsidies in the future.

Areas for Resolution

The upcoming negotiations should continue the work begun in the Uruguay Round and eliminate existing export subsidies. There is no economic justification for their continued use. By removing subsidised exports, world prices should increase, and farmers, particularly in the EU, will not be artificially encouraged to overproduce products that they cannot grow competitively.

In addition to eliminating export subsidies, countries should examine the rules defining export subsidies to ensure that countries do not resort to other policy tools that might allow governments to distort markets. Specially, WTO members should look closely at curbing agricultural state trading export monopolies that can exert undue market power or dispose of surplus commodies on a non-market basis. A recent WTO victory by the United States and New Zealand over Canada's special-class system of dairy exports shows that the existing rule against circumvention are effective but must be enforced.

Export credit and food aid programmes were addressed in the Uruguay Round agreement in recognition of the fact that those tools could be disguised as subsidies. These policies may again be on the agenda when the WTO negotiations commence next time. It will be important to ensure that the world's needy continue to have access to imported products, even when financial turmoil rolls world markets and limits the ability of developing countries to meet their food and fiber needs.

Certain large exporting nations—primarily in the EU have used export taxes as a supply management tool by intervening in the market to restrict exports when domestic stocks are low. These measures can wreak havoc in international markets, exacerbating price swings and reducing the confidence of net-food-importing countries to abandon trade barriers and rely on the international market to provide food security. Similarly, some exporting countries use differential export taxes to discourage exports of basic products (such as grains or oilseeds); they force exporters to process the product domestically (into flour or oil and meal, for example) and export the value added products.

21

Add Value, Go Global

Can Southern Firms Break into Export Markets?

The global economy has changed beyond recognition over the last decade. Widespread economic policy reform and in particular trade liberalisation have opened up new opportunities for developing countries. In poor countries, however, the consequences of trade liberalisation are not always positive. What can the private sector do to respond better and make the most of new trading opportunities? What factors have limited the impact of economic reforms on export performance?

Why have exports from poorer countries failed to increase more rapidly following trade liberalisation? What can be done to improve performance? Research on the response of firms in the private sector to economic reform can underpin new approaches to export promotion for poorer developing countries. For a long time, protective trade policies, poorly performing state-owned industries and state controls over the private sector were blamed for poor export performance in Africa and South Asia. Now that some of these problems have been remedied, other obstacles have come to light.

The effect of economic liberalisation and adjustment on the performance of poor countries has been cause for concern. Trade liberalisation should increase incentives to export and facilitate business enterprise by encouraging private ownership through privatisation and by attracting foreign investment. Macro-economic stability ought to boost business confidence and performance. All these factors should promote exports, offsetting job and income losses caused by the closure or reorganisation of inefficient enterprises and industries yet, although some degree of reform and stability it is without export growth that was expected.

Trade reform and macro-economic stability may be necessary conditions for improved export performance put by them are insufficient. The obstacles to improving export performance are numerous and there is no easy policy answer. The research programme examined export performance at three levels.

- *Regional:* How trade strategies should vary with skills and natural resource endowments
- *National:* Factors influencing the export performance of manufacturing
- *Sectoral:* The performance of particular sectors of the economy.

The East Asian economies have shown that developing countries can complete successfully in global markets. For many, they provide a blueprint for economic growth applicable to many poor countries.

South Asia's comparative advantage lies in its abundant unskilled labour, while Africa's lies in its abundant natural resources. Different export promotion strategies are essential. South Asia's best prospectus are in labour-intensive manufacturing: the region's low level of exports would soar over the next decade if current obstacles to trade were reduced. Africa's exports could also increase but its biggest potential in primary products that need little educated labour and abundant natural resources.

Some African countries could also be substantial exporters of manufacturers, but their actual manufactured exports in most cases now fall far short. Comparing Ghana to Mauritius—one of Africa's most successful exporters of manufactured goods differences in firm-level efficiency are apparent Mauritian firms have more capital per worker and use it more efficiently. Reducing trade barriers is not sufficient. Wages in Ghana would have to be substantially lower to offset low labour productivity. Alternatively, labour productivity will have to be drastically improved if Ghanian firms are to compete successfully in export markets with wages at current levels.

Even when companies use capital and labour efficiently, poor infrastructure is a frequent stumbling products to export markets—an acute problem in landlocked countries and equally acute for manufacturers as research on Uganda clearly shows. What huts manufacturing exporters is being hit by the high cost of transporting their output to foreign markets and of transporting the materials they need from abroad. The cost penalties resulting from geography and poor infrastructure are far greater in Uganda than from high tariffs and other import restrictions.

Southern firms can still break into export markets, however, developing-country firms do export to markets with exacting standards for product quality, reliability of delivery, and consumer safety. Two crucial aspects, however, are often overlooked:

- Non-manufacturing sectors, such as tourism and horticulture, generate significant employment and offer opportunities for supplying increasingly sophisticated products. Although manufacturing is considered more attractive, certain areas of tourism and horticulture can be equally appealing.

- New export opportunities are created as southern producers establish closer links with foreign customers. Producers of labour-intensive products such as garments, horticulture and footwear frequently depend on large retailers and specialist international traders for designs, information about demand and technical support.

Supermarkets make key decisions about which fruits and vegetables to grow, how they should be produced and processed and which firms should be included in the business. Strategic decisions by international producers and retailers in the footwear industry have been crucial in developing new production locations such as Vietnam and Romania. Similarly, work on automotive components production in South Africa and India illustrates how global sourcing by the leading motor companies closes off some markets and opens up others. Export prospects can only be evaluated in the light of global restructuring in these industries.

Emphasising global linkages does not mean that developing countries are powerless in the face of global forces. Even in tightly-structured industries, there is scope for national policy and national strategy. Further more, there are important export sectors that are not structured in this way. Some tourism is dominated by large northern firms and is heavily import-dependent, but there is also enormous potential and national policy will be crucial in shaping the industry and its contribution to the economy as a whole.

For southern firms to break into export markets, certain issues must be addressed, especially in Africa. Some are recognised as important policy issues—investing in human capital and improving infrastructure for example. As one set of constraints are reduced—such as removing policy—induced distortions through trade liberalisation—another set takes precedence. In response to the integration of global markets, southern producers must join the global distribution chains to ensure markets for their exports.

These findings impose hard choice on developing countries. Should a firm allocate limited funds for investment in human capital or investment infrastructure? Future research might contribute by quantifying relative rates of return. On another level, countries may worry about the independence and autonomy of local producers if they are to join a global chain typically donated by northern companies. Rules regulate governmental trade and investment policies but who controls the global buyers and multinational companies whose decisions have such huge impacts on developing countries?

22

Revisiting Bretton Woods

Reforming the World Trade and Finance System

That leading trio of major multilateral economic institutions (The International Monetary Fund and World Bank in Washington D.C. and the WTO in Geneva) were created from the ashes of World War II to build a strong, coordinated, international set of economic arrangements. They did well. Their contributions significantly forges systems of cooperation between governments which, in turn, encouraged global economic growth and development.

But, is it time now to revisit Bretton Woods, that location in the hills of New Hampshire, where half a century ago U.S. Treasury Secretary Harry Dexter White, British Economist Lord Keynes, and many others, set the plans for the post-war multilateral economic system?

The question is not academic. It was being asked recently in an unprecedented scale in the annual meeting of the IMF and World Bank in Washington D.C. The questioning came for three critical reasons:

First, there is a widespread view that a strong supranational institution is urgently required in the currency arena. The IMF has been absorbed with medium-term economics assistance programmes and appears to be attaching low priority to its original purpose. The IMF's Articles of Agreement declare the Fund's purpose is: "To promote international monetary cooperation through a permanent institution which provides the machinery for consultation and collaboration on international monetary problems".

Second, the WTO has brought tempers to the boil in many developing countries and created fears. The WTOs failure is serving now as a stimulus for the growth of regional trade blocs, based upon major industrial countries and open to relatively few developing countries.

Third, the World Bank has taken a backseat when it has come to advancing Western support for the poorest nations. There was a time when the President of the World Bank would use his office to rally international opinion and publicly urge the industrial nations to take a more constructive and more generous approach to the developing nations. In recent times the leadership of the institution has been silent. It has become mired in administrative matters, willing to bow to IMF leadership and content to seek to influence development thinking through the publication of economic research reports.

World Bank Subordinate to IMF

At the same time, the World Bank has come to play second fiddle to the IMF. The Fund has engineered itself into a position of leadership in economic policy discussion with developing countries and with the former command economies of East Europe and Central Asia. The World Bank does not provide programme lending of any kind until a borrowing country first has an IMF programme in place. While the two institutions are totally distinct in legal and financial terms, the Bank has accepted a subordinate position to the IMF.

These three phenomena are not encouraging for the health of global economy and from the perspective, in particular, of the developing countries.

On the monetary front there is a need to protect the interests of developing and emerging countries from the vagaries of the super-economic powers. Most of the governments of the world have looked on hopelessly as Japan,

Germany and the United States, have pursued nationalist economic policies that have played havoc with the currency system. Most of the world's trade is booked in the currencies of these countries and when those currencies spin out of control, so concluding trade deals and securing investment agreements becomes far more complex.

Uncertainty and instability in the world's currency systems are menaces that the IMF was expressly designed to counter. But the IMF has become so engaged in development lending (it now talks of providing programmes to some 80 countries) that its need for financial resources of its own is growing rapidly. That need makes it difficult for the Fund to be critical of its most powerful members. It cannot bite the hands that feed it. Thus, calls to the major nations for fiscal restraint, monetary discipline and international cooperation are made in muted tones.

The Fund, however, must respond to the mounting recognition that some supranational mechanisms are needed to survey the international economic landscape, to ring the alarm bells, to push and shove for meaningful consultation and to place blame on those whose policies are so nationalistic that they endanger the international system. IMF surveillance of the major economic power needs teeth.

The Fund should concentrate once again on using its influence and its expert staff to enhance international understanding of the complexities of the global trading and financial system. By this means it can rebuild its influence with the major powers. While it is unrealistic at this juncture to call for the IMF to become the world's central bank, it could serve as a vitally important convenor of consultative processes designed to attain the objectives that its founders decreed: "To facilitate the expansion and balanced growth of international trade, and to contribute thereby to the promotion and maintenance of high levels of employment and real income and to the development of the productive resources of all members as primary objectives of economic policy".

The IMF's role should be enhanced. It should blend its monetary miles with new trade roles. The WTO been the forum for negotiations and for the supervisions of agreements. WTO does not undertake projects, it does not have powers to influence the policies of its most powerful members and it does not have the prestige needed to provide real leadership. It is time that the WTO was merged into the IMF.

Trade and Finance Belong Together

It makes little sense to split issues of international capital flows from trade questions. The globalisation of trade and investment has brought these disciplines close together. If forging satisfactory agreements is often difficult, then this in part is due to the fact that distinct organisations have leadership for distinct parts (WTO for trade and IMF for money) and there is no effective mechanism for cooperation. It is also the case that within national governments the trade and finance ministries are often in conflict and face insufficient pressure to coordinate. If the IMF managed both trade and monetary negotiations on the global scale, then this would add pressures on trade and finance ministers to work together.

Returning to its original monetary roles and adding a major trade role should be more than enough to keep the IMF busy. It would be logical, particularly in such circumstances, that the Fund return to the World Bank the development financing roles that it has assumed in recent years and that diverted it from its original purposes.

The IMF's Articles stress that one of its purposes is "to give confidence to members by making the general resources of the Fund temporarily available to them under adequate safeguards, thus providing them with opportunity to correct maladjustments in their balance of payments without resorting to measures destructive of national or international prosperity".

The Fund might argue that the World Bank should confine itself to infrastructure and social project finance and technical assistance and leave all programme lending to the IMF. The reality is that the World Bank discovered to an increasing degrees, starting with experiences with Turkey in 1979 and then with many highly indebted nations from 1982 onwards, that the best development projects will fail in countries where wholly unsatisfactory economic policies are in place. The Bank has also recognised the pain and complexity of adjustment and that countries embarking on adjustment policies enter upon a multi-year process: a process better geared to types of financing arrangements that the World Bank can offer, than those provided by the IMF.

Avoid Duplication of Effort between IMF and World Bank

The experiences of the last decade have strengthened the World Bank's understanding of macro-economic policy reform and enhanced its capacity to provide comprehensive policy from support to its member countries. Cooperation with the IMF has improved, but it is also second best option and an expensive one. There remains too much duplication between the Fund and the Bank. The biggest cost is paid by the borrowing countries—ministers and their immediate subordinates spend endless hours negotiating separately with IMF and World Bank teams and developing duplicative reports.

Reform is only necessary when things are not working well. Today there is enormous scope for improvement in the global trading, monetary and development areas. The three prime institutions created for these areas are not performing well enough. Reform is urgent: the WTO should be merged with the IMF, the IMF should refocus on issues fundamental to securing a healthy global monetary (and trading) system and withdraw from the aid game: and the World Bank should have enlarged scope and provide more leadership on the development front.

Such reforms will not end the problems that our world economic system faces and their significance will be largely determined by the support they receive from the leaders of the most powerful industrial nations, irrespective of the zeal of the officials within the IMF and World Bank. Today, in the midst of prolonged international slump where nobody is satisfied with the ways in which the international system is operating, there is an important opportunity to secure backing in the capitals of the world's super-economic powers for the types of reform that are articulated here.

23

Give Developing Countries A More Favourable Deal

An Assessment of the World Trade Conference in Doha

At the end of the 4th WTO Ministerial Conference in Doha, Qatar, the representatives of all WTO member states vigorously applauded Director-General Mike Moore when he dubbed the adopted work programmes for the new round of trade negotiations the "Doha development agenda."

The launching of a new round of trade negotiations with a broad agenda was the objective persistently pursued by the industrial countries, in particular the European Union, the United States, Canada and Japan. This objective has been achieved. Besides the continuation of the negotiations in the fields of agriculture and services, the Ministerial Declaration adopted by the Conference provides for the opening of negotiations in eleven additional fields. Undoubtedly a success for the industrial countries.

Clear Mandate for a New Development Round

The negotiating mandate, though, clearly reflects the political will to make the new round a "development round" with the aim of significantly improving the integration of the developing countries into the world trading system. To a large extent it takes into account the specific interests of the developing countries. Certainly a success with which the developing countries can credit themselves. A crucial factor for the course and the successful outcome of the Ministerial Conference was, without doubt, the active involvement of the developing countries in the preparatory and negotiating process.

Doha Determines Merely the Work Programme for Negotiations

The Ministerial Declaration adopted at the conference merely determines the work programme for the new round of trade negotiations. Three factors contributed decisively to the positive outcome of the Ministerial Conference. There was a broad consensus among the WTO members states that (*i*) a second Seattle-like failure would put the WTO's workability at risk and was to be avoided at all costs (the 3rd WTO Ministerial Conference I Seattle in December 1999 ended in chaos without the adoption of a Ministerial Declaration); (*ii*) the recessionary trends in the world economy were to be countered with the successful conclusion of the Ministerial Conference in Doha to improve the prospect for short-term recovery and, thereafter, sustained economic growth; (*iii*) in response to the terrorist attacks of September 11, 2001, there should be a clear commitment to strengthen the rules-based multilateral trading system. Failure was, therefore, not an option. The strategic conclusion drawn from the Seattle failure was to limit the Doha Ministerial Declaration to establishing a broad, generally-worded negotiating mandate for a new round of trade talks that does not anticipate the outcome of the negotiations on controversial issues. The strategy worked. The deliberations at the Ministerial Conference focussed on the scope of the negotiating mandate. The task of reconciling the conflicting interests between industrial and developing countries and working out a fair compromise has been left to the forthcoming negotiations.

Recognition of the Interests of the Developing Countries

In view of the objective of creating a basis for sustained economic growth in the developing countries by better integrating them into the world economy and increasing their share in world trade, important preliminary decisions with regard to the forthcoming negotiations were taken by the Ministerial Conference:

- The Ministerial Declaration stresses the importance of implementing and interpreting the Agreement on Trade-Related Aspects of Intellectual Property Rights (TRIPS Agreement) in a manner supportive of public health and access to medicines; in recognition of the seriousness of the problem, a separate 'Declaration on the TRIPS Agreement and Public Health' was adopted; a number of public-health related issues have been referred to the Council for TRIPS for further deliberation;

- The Council for TRIPS has been tasked to examine the relationship between (*i*) the TRIPS Agreement and the Convention on Biological Diversity and (*ii*) the protection of traditional knowledge, taking full account of the development dimension;

- Numerous problems regarding the implementation of WTO agreements are dealt with in a separate 'Decision on Implementation-Related Issues and Concerns' adopted by the Ministerial Conference; outstanding implementation issues are to be addressed as a matter of priority by the relevant WTO bodies;

- The Council for Trade in Goods will examine the proposal to bring forward the liberalisation of the textile sector under the Agreement on Textiles and Clothing;

- As regards agriculture, comprehensive negotiations were agreed on, aiming at substantial improvements in market access; reductions of, with a view to phasing out, all forms of export subsidies; and substantial reductions in trade-distorting domestic support;

- As regards market access for non-agricultural goods, negotiations were agreed on, with the aim of reducing or, as appropriate, eliminating tariffs and non-tariff trade barriers in particular on products of export interest to developing countries;

- Recognition of the principle of special and differential treatment of the developing countries as an integral part of all WTO agreements;
- Technical cooperation and capacity building have been recognised in the Ministerial Declaration as 'core elements of the development dimension of the multilateral trading system' and firm commitments have been established in various paragraphs.

Turning the Ministerial Declaration's Spirit into Practical Policy

With these preliminary decisions regarding the agenda of the forthcoming negotiations, the course is set for the better integration of the developing countries into the world economy. To stay the course, there must be clear commitment and political will on the part of the industrial countries to make the new round a 'development round' by taking the developing countries' interest fully into account, being prepared to make meaningful concessions, and making good on the promise of significantly increased trade and investment-related technical assistance.

In the course of the negotiations it might prove a problem that many of the obligations in favour of the developing countries are formulated rather vaguely. The Ministerial Declaration is confined to declarations of intent even where—with a certain degree of goodwill—binding commitments would have been politically feasible. The bringing forward of the liberalisation of the textile sector, a key demand of the developing countries, has been referred to the Council for Trade in Goods for examination; this is certainly an expression of the industrial countries' willingness to compromise, but it in no way anticipates the final decision. As regards the objective of duty-free and quota-free access for all products of the least developed countries to the markets of the industrial countries the Ministerial Declaration simply repeats the commitment which was already expressed in the United Nations Millennium Declaration of September 2000, at the 3rd United

Nations Conference on Least Developed Countries in Brussels in May 2001, and at the G7/8 Summit in Genoa in July 2001. Except for the European Union, no party has put this commitment into practice so far; the United States and Japan in particular have shown little enthusiasm for introducing duty-free and quota-free access of all LDC products.

What makes us believe that the Doha Ministerial Declaration will make a difference? The chapter on agriculture is more specific in that it provides for negotiations aimed at significantly improved market access, reductions/phasing out of all forms of export subsidies, and substantial reductions in trade-distorting domestic support. However, a clear road map including a timetable for the negotiations and specific benchmarks for the reduction targets were beyond Doha's reach; in addition, the qualifier that the commitment to comprehensive negotiations does not prejudge the outcome of these negotiations leaves a back door open. In conclusion: if you remove the merely rhetorical phrases—such as "we place the developing countries' needs and interests at the heart of the World Programme adopted in this Declaration", "to take fully into account the development dimension...", —from the Ministerial Declaration, it becomes quite clear that the text contains relatively few 'programming elements' with a view to the development agenda of the forthcoming negotiations.

Fears that the vested interests of the industrial countries will re-gain precedence over development aspects in the course of the negotiating process are certainly not entirely baseless. The 'steel war' the United States is about to declare on the rest of the world clearly indicates that the Doha fair weather period is over. Business as usual has returned. The American steel tariff threats prompted EU Trade Commissioner Pascal Lamy to speak of a "perverse signal at a time when the ink is barely dry on the Doha Agreement."

The non-governmental organisations have a decisive role to play. It is their role to monitor the new round of trade negotiations, to make the negotiating process more transparent, to create public awareness with regard to the issues at stake, and to build up political pressure with the objective of making sure that development aspects are not pushed to one side and that the interest of the developing countries will make their way into the agreements to be concluded.

Coherence of Trade Policy and Development Policy

The negotiating mandate for the new round of trade talks adopted in Doha has brought development politics onto the agenda of the WTO. The mention of development aspects in the WTO set of rules and regulations is not, in essence, new. In fact, the development dimension is recognised as an integral part of the general WTO mandate to foster economic growth. However, the particular importance the Doha Ministerial Declaration attaches to the consideration of development aspects in the negotiation process (it seeks, as it is put there, "to place the developing countries' needs and interests at the heart of the work programme") offers the opportunity to achieve greater coherence of trade policy and development policy. In this respect, the Doha Ministerial Declaration reflects the same trend as the "Everthing-but-Arms-Initiative" (EBA) of the European Union. Subsequent to its adoption by the EU member states, Pascal Lamy emphasised the coherence aspect as the characteristic feature of EBA initiative (outweighing the shortcomings relating to bananas, rice, and sugar) by saying, "It is the first time that the European Union's trade policy has been substantially modified by the necessity of contributing to development policy." This perspective also characterised the 3rd United Nations Conference on Least Developed Countries in Brussels in May 2001.

To sum up, it can be said that the Doha conference has sent out an important signal for the process of coordinating trade and development policy with the long-term objective of achieving a coherent policy framework. The next step towards greater coherency can be taken at the International Conference on Financing for Development in Monterrey/Mexico in March 2002.

Sustainable Development as the Guideline for Further Developing the Multilateral Trading System

The Ministerial Declaration reaffirms the commitment to the objective of sustainable development, as stated in the preamble to the Marrakesh Agreement of April 1994 (i.e. the Agreement establishing the WTO). However, theory and practice are far apart. The negotiating mandate for the new round is too cautious a step towards integrating environmental and social aspects into the WTO set of rules and regulations to be able to bridge that gap. Looking at the three pillars of the sustainable development concept—economic development, environmental protection, and social protection—, in a nutshell the following can be said:

The negotiating mandate for the new round deserves good grades as far as the first pillar, economic development, is concerned. The course is set for better integration of the developing countries into the multilateral trading system, thus giving them the chance of actually benefiting from further trade liberalisation in the form of trade-induced economic growth. The inclusion of the so-called 'Singapore issues', investment and competition, offers the prospect of a medium-to long-term improvement of the business and investment climate in the developing countries. As for environmental protection, negotiations on a (very) limited scale have been agreed on, the desirability of further negotiations will be examined. This is certainly not a big breakthrough, but a first step towards integrating ecological aspects into the trade rules. Disappointingly (but not surprisingly), social issues were not dealt with at the Doha Ministerial Conference. The developing countries' resistance to even discussing social issues, such as core labour standards, in the framework of the WTO could not be overcome; the issue was considered an absolute 'deal-breaker'.

Outlook

The developing countries' consent to the launching of a new round of trade talks cannot disguise the fact that there are still significant differences of opinion over a number of issues, including such key issues as agriculture, environment, investment and competition, and that there is a great deal of mistrust on the part of the developing countries. The one-day extension of the Ministerial Conference alone is proof of how difficult the process of reaching consensus on the launching of a new round of trade talks and its agenda had been. In order to successfully conclude the new round, the industrial countries have to deliver on their commitments, such as improving market access for goods of export interest to the developing countries and increasing their trade-related technical assistance.

The assurance of increased technical assistance was a major bargaining chip in getting the development countries' OK for the new round. If insufficient funds for technical assistance and capacity building measures are provided, it will most certainly diminish the chances of getting quick results. In a comment on the forthcoming negotiations, the British Economist also highlighted the credibility aspect and the need for significant concessions, "Poor countries remain deeply suspicious of the rich world's commitment to truly freer trade. They bitterly remember the Uruguay Round, whose benefits went mostly to the rich. For the new talks to succeed, those suspicions must be proven wrong. Europe and America must quickly open up their markets for farm products and textiles. They must show that environmental concerns are not going to become a backdoor excuse for renewed protectionism. They must reform their oft-abused system of anti-dumping rules. And they must deliver on promises to beef up poorer countries' capacity to deal with the intricate procedures in the world trading system."

The Doha Ministerial Declaration offers the prospect of long-term gains for the developing countries. However, turning potential into actual gains requires tenacity in pursuing policies aimed at improving the business climate and, in general, the framework conditions for economic growth. Increased trade-related technical assistance and improved market access will not automatically result in growing export volumes for the developing countries. In addition, the strengthening and diversification of productive capacity is required. Successful integration into the global economy depends on tackling the supply-side constraints and other 'behind-the border impediments to trade' (ranging from weak infrastructure, insufficient ancillary services and poor governance to macro-economic instability). The Tanzanian Trade Minister, Iddi Simba, emphasised the complexity of the problems the developing countries are facing in his statement at the Ministerial Conference: "To operationalise the development agenda we need to have adequate capacity building which will go beyond addressing the normal WTO obligations. Adequate resources in the form of financial and technology transfer need to be in place to address the supply-side constraints. Along the same lines, WTO Director-General Mike Moore stated, "Capacity problems [in producing goods and services competitively], not trade barriers, are the major obstacles to growth in developing countries."

Concluding Remark

By creating a rules-based multilateral trading system, the WTO set of rules and regulations contributes to the shaping of the process of globalisation and to the emerging system of global governance. However, it can hardly be disputed that so far the industrial countries have been the main beneficiaries of the WTO-driven economic globalisation. We are still miles away from a true win-win situation. In a recent interview with the German weekly *Die Zeit*, the, Nigerian President, Olusegun Obasanjo, criticised the industrial countries' hypocrisy, saying "Globalisation is a good thing. But only if there is a level playing field, from which all countries are able to benefit. You tell us that we have to open up our markets for your goods, whereas you keep your markets closed for our goods. Europe protects itself with innumerable trade barriers, everybody knows that. What kind of rules are those?"

That is exactly what matters. The new round of trade negotiations launched in Doha must result in modified trade rules. Trade rules which take account of the specific economic constraints of the developing countries and are more favourable to them. The developing countries must be given the chance to 'cash in' on trade liberalisation and, strengthened by trade-induced economic growth, to pursue national pro-poor policies aimed at eradicating poverty.

24

The Trade-related Intellectual Property Rights (TRIPS) Agreement and the Developing Countries

The basic norms of free competition established in the nineteenth century induced legislators to provide relatively weak forms of intellectual property protection. Often innovators could rely only on such factors as lead time, reputation for quality and continuing technical improvements to maintain their foothold in the market.

Undermining this outlook were two developments that led to the inclusion of intellectual property issues in the World Trade Organisation (WTO). First, the rise of knowledge-based industries radically altered the nature of competition and disrupted the equilibrium that had resulted from more traditional comparative advantages. Second, the growing capacity of manufacturers in developing countries to penetrate distant markets for traditional industrial products forced the developed countries to rely more heavily on their comparative advantages in the production of intellectual goods than in the past. Market access for developing countries thus became a bargaining chip to be exchanged for greater protection of intellectual goods within a restructured global marketplace.

Since 1986 the developed countries' drive for extraterritorial protection of intellectual property rights has largely ignored the competitive capabilities of developing countries with respect to intellectual goods, and it has also downplayed these countries' rights to preferential treatment under existing rules. At the same time, the logic of multilateral trade negotiations skews the pre-existing North-South conflict over intellectual property rights by introducing the prospects of trade concessions in unrelated fields. Intellectual property rights constitute but one of many variables that bear on competitive capacity and the transfer of technology in general.

Primary Intellectual Property Regimes

Patents

The extension of patentability to virtually all types of technology recognised by developed patent systems, the prolongation of patent protection to a uniform term of twenty years, and legal recognition of the patentee's exclusive rights to import the relevant products could adversely affect developing countries whose existing patent laws fall below these standards. In practice, however, the competitive status of any given developing country in a post-TRIPS world will depend in part on the level of foreign direct investment it attracts and on the benefits that strengthened intellectual property rights bring to domestic innovators.

Competition under stronger patent regimes requires developing countries to adopt legal means of narrowing the scope of foreign patent monopolies and of encouraging local entrepreneurs either to work around the claimed inventions or to develop improvements suited to local conditions. To this end, local entrepreneurs should exploit technical information in disclosures published abroad; patent authorities should exercise all of the claims limitations practised abroad; and domestic courts should strictly interpret the doctrine of equivalents. Legislative enactment of utility model laws would provide additional incentives to adapt foreign inventions to local conditions and to improve them further.

Moreover, unpatented traditional technologies will often remain suitable for local needs, and the resulting products may be sold at lower prices than imported products of patented technologies. Entrepreneurs in developing countries should also be prepared to exploit unpatented applications of applied scientific know-how in such advanced technologies as biogenetic engineering and computer programme-related innovation.

In time, increased direct investment by foreign patentees could enable developing-country licensees who exploit their natural advantages, especially low labour costs, to succeed on both domestic and export markets where non-licensees were unable or unwilling to venture in the past. Familiarisation with the benefits of the patent system should stimulate greater investment in domestic research and development and in technological innovation.

The gradual extension of patents to new technologies such as computer programmes and bio-genetic engineering without the emergence of agreed international minimum standards creates both opportunities and risks for the developing countries. While the developed countries enjoy unique advantages in biotechnology that only become available to developing countries as a consequence of stronger patent systems, some developing countries may find their own competitive status enhanced by the provision of proprietary rights, including plant breeders' rights, though others may not. The patenting of biogenetic advances decreases the scope for reverse-engineering and could also increase the costs of doing business in key sectors of some developing economies, notably agriculture. As regards information technologies, reliance on copyright and trade secrets at the international level appears less unfavourable to the developing countries' prospects than patents, for reasons that are set out below. However, the tendency to patent software could diminish these prospects by posing limits to reverse engineering and to the attainment of the interoperability, and this trend adds to the overall costs of disseminating information goods.

To the extent that patented technology is not made available on reasonable terms or that un-wholesome economic dependencies actually arise, developing countries will have to consider measures to restore the competitive balance that are consistent with the TRIPS Agreement. For example, the agreement allows compulsory licences when the rights holders fail to licences patented technology "on reasonable commercial terms". It also provides other bases for defensive regulatory action by emphasizing "the transfer and dissemination of technology, to the mutual advantage of producers and users" and the need "to promote the public interest in sectors of vital importance to socio-economic and technological development".

Measures to restrain abuse of intellectual property rights as authorised by the Paris Convention also remain available under the TRIPS agreement, which expressly empowers developing countries to deal with licensing practices that "adversely affect the international transfer of technology".

Finally, the agreement specifically preserves the right of all states to "adopt measures necessary to protect public health and nutrition and to promote the public interest in sectors of vital importance to socio-economic and technological development, provided that such measures are consistent with the provisions of this agreement".

Trade-marks and Geographical Indications

The TRIPS provisions give pre-existing norms greater specificity while softening the use requirement and eliminating both compulsory licences and local linkage requirements. These provisions also subject the international regime of trade-marks and unfair competition to more stringent enforcement measures, including border controls against imports of counterfeit goods.

As a result, developing countries will need to reassess the pro-competitive functions of trade marks in open economies while addressing questions of abuse in a more direct fashion. They should insist on receiving the technical cooperation and aid that the TRIPS agreement envisages for the purpose of defraying administrative and enforcement burdens.

Governments should consider policies and incentives that encourage enterprises to establish their own market identities through appropriate trade-marks and foreign firms to allow licensees to adopt more of the licenced products for both domestic and export needs under local trade-marks.

Copyrights

Authors in many developing countries are very active in both domestic and foreign markets. It nonetheless remains true that the balance of trade in cultural goods favours exports from developed countries. This imbalance could increase under the TRIPS agreement, which generally applies the international minimum standards of the Berne Convention, plus selected standards from the Rome Convention on neighbouring rights.

While efforts to implement these standards is mandatory, developing-country authorities should familiarize themselves with the extent to which the scope of copyright protection varies from country to country, in the absence of authoritative legal limitations recognised by international law. Carefully framed public-interest exceptions may further reduce the overall costs of a TRIPS Agreement without violating international copyright norms. Moreover, the revised Berne Convention already provides for compulsory licences for educational and scientific test, and developing countries may wish to consider making greater use of these concessions.

Ancillary Proprietary Regimes

Trade Secrets

In modern economies trade secret law regulates the pace of competition by endowing second comers with an absolute right to reverse-engineer. To operate successfully under such a regime, developing countries must realign the concept of "transfer of technology" with the nature of competition in open markets. Technology is transferred through self-help methods of reverse engineering. The potential benefits of reverse-engineering unpatented technologies increase when advanced technologies are involved, notably biogenetic engineering, computer programmes and computer-aided design. The unpatented, non-copyrightable know-how underlying these technologies is often embodied in tangible products available to the public, which renders classical trade secret protection of doubtful efficacy. By ignoring this problem, the TRIPS Agreement provides entrepreneurs in developing countries with major opportunities, notwithstanding the extension of trade secret law under TRIPS, provided they are willing and able to master the art of reverse-engineering.

Other Proprietary Regimes

The TRIPS Agreement mandates intellectual property protection for industrial designs, plant varieties and integrated circuit designs. Although the developed countries enjoy a clear advantage in advanced sectors of industrial design, more traditional sectors rooted in aesthetic appeal rather than technical efficiency remain accessible to firms in developing countries.

Need for Multilateral Policies

Global economic integration increasingly requires that intangible creations receive minimum international standards of legal protection. Purely territorial intellectual property rights will thus give way to international sovereignty. However, the norms of that law represent a delicate balance between the interests of States at different stages of development, so that the evolution of international intellectual property law will have to accommodate these norms and that balance.

Efforts to implement higher intellectual property standards will put increasing strains on competition law, which is not directly covered by the TRIPS Agreement.

Identifying the parameters of healthy competition valid for all players in an integrated world market will become a pressing task for the international community in a post-TRIPS world. These issues will be complicated by the fact that innovators, users and second comers all have different stakes in fashioning the rules of unfair competition law, and their interests will increasingly vary more with their economic roles than with the geopolitical affiliations of their respective national States.

Competition law must, become an integral part of international discussions of intellectual property rights, and there is a great need for multilateral cooperation to achieve a marketwide balance between incentives to create, and reasonable opportunities to imitate and improve upon, technological innovation. These discussions should lead to an internationally agreed framework for promoting a transfer of technology that is compatible with the drive for greater economic efficiency. To the extent that such cooperation succeeds, it will contribute a new perspective to the notion of fair competition that should strengthen the prospects of all participants in the global marketplace.

25

New Agenda of the WTO

One "new" issue that is already in the WTO work programme is the relationship between trade and the environment. At the heart of the matter is how to relate the rules-based multilateral trade system, continued trade liberalisation and further development of the global economy to environmental concerns and objectives. It is possible to envisage circumstances in which trade, unsupported by sound environmental policy, could involve damage to the environment—or, on the contrary, in which environmental regulations could harm legitimate trade. In such circumstances, however, careful judgment is necessary in weighing whether it is trade policy or environmental policy which must be adjusted, it is also not difficult to see how ill-considered international environmental agreement could needlessly frustrate trade and reduce incomes and even put risk environmental reform and improvement. At the same time, it is just as important to recognize the circumstances in which, by encouraging efficiency and a better allocation of scarce resources, trade liberalisation may be supportive of an improved environment. The WTO will contribute to a better understanding of the issues, and assist governments in developing more coherent policies in this area.

Trade and investment is leading candidate for the new agenda, since one of the consequences of globalisation is to lessen the distinctions among different forms of market access. In the GATT framework, market access simply in terms of tariffs and non-tariff measures. Reducing tariffs and eliminating other trade barriers at the frontier was the recipe for liberalisation. Foreign investment was an altogether different matter. Indeed, countries often used to regard tariffs and other trade barriers as convenient mechanisms for inducing foreign investment. Protection of the domestic market offered attractive profits to foreign investors. This was the essence of the import substitution development strategy—a strategy that in large measure failed and has now been discredited. In today's world of international business, trade and investment are increasingly viewed as complements, not substitutes. Different parts of internationally-based businesses can be located in several different countries. Increasingly, businesses trade to invest, and invest to trade. The WTO cannot afford to concern itself only with the trade side of the equation—that would be to deny the reality of modern global business practices.

It is not coincidence that foreign direct investment flows worldwide quadrupled, to almost US $200 billion per annum, in the ten years to 1993. Indeed, the importance of investment was recognised in the General Agreement on Trade in Services negotiated in the Uruguay Round, where investment, or commercial presence, was one of the four modes of service supply in respect of which WTO members undertook market access commitments. But there is a need for a broader, or more horizontal approach to international investment rules. Such rules would build on the WTO principles of non-discrimination and national treatment, and create a policy environment to encourage and safeguard foreign investment, whether in goods or services.

Governments will increasingly recognize the need for work on investment in a more global setting as well. Especially so since developing countries are not only the target of a growing proportion of international investment but are themselves becoming important overseas investors. One should note that the Uruguay Round Agreement on Trade-related Investment Measures calls for an examination by members within five years of the case for developing provisions on investment policy.

That same mandate refers to competition policy, which also has to be examined as a possible candidate for further work. Of course, what has done in the GATT and the WTO over 50 years in promoting a liberal trading environment is precisely the enhancement of competition. But if we have succeeded in getting the rules of competition between countries to work effectively, that very success requires us to go further and consider how the behaviour of companies can serve to distort international competition. The need to see whether there are any areas where explicit competition rules, or specific understandings, are necessary internationally to complement the statutes that many governments already have on their books. There is no doubt that competition rules are essential to the proper functioning of markets—the need to clarify, however, is how best to promote such disciplines, both nationally and internationally.

Trade and Social Standards: This is a highly controversial issue, and in the absence of a consensus there is no possibility that it could be brought into the agenda of the WTO. It is clear that what the need first and foremost is a comprehensive effort to bring some clarity to the many complex issues that are involved here.

The first issue to be clarified is the nature of the subject; talking about the comparative advantage of developing countries which comes from lower wage level—as the issue is sometimes presented—or talking about human rights or labour standard? It is fundamentally important to clarify the terms of the debate as it relates to trade. The second point is to identify what are the key issues related to trade; for example, talking about child labour or trade union rights in terms of labour standards or in terms of human rights? There are just some of the preconditions for opening a discussion on whether a useful debate is, in fact, possible on these issues. One of these principles is that economic and social growth and development are to a large extent interdependent. When the economic situation is poor, the social situation is also likely to be poor. And correspondingly, where there is economic growth, social development is more likely to come too.

While no-one should challenge the legitimate right of developing countries to use the comparative advantage of lower costs, and no-one should use human rights and issues of social standards as an excuse for disguised protectionism, no country should deliberately deny workers' rights or attempt to generate artificially-lower costs by forced labour, discrimination against women, exploitation of children or other such abuses.

No one should on no account allow this debate to re-open a North-South divide. Dialogue is the best approach to finding ways to improve the observance of labour standards. In order to convince developing countries that no protectionist considerations are involved in the debate, it is essential to prove that all possible measures other than trade sanctions are being taken to alleviate the problems. One excellent example is the Memorandum of Understanding on the elimination of child labour from the garments industry in Bangladesh that was signed in July 1995 by the industry, the ILO and UNICEF, with support from the Bangladesh and US Governments. This joint approach combines restrictions on child labour with the improvement of educational opportunities for the children involved. This is a targeted and constructive approach to a specific problem, and as such it offers a useful model for future efforts. On the other hand, to simply restrict imports of garments from the industries concerned would in all likelihood have just worsened the situation of these children.

Reciprocity and Regionalism

Reciprocity and the growth of regionalism in international trade relations is very important. There are from to time calls for trade policies based on reciprocity instead of the basic "Most Favoured Nations" (MFN) principle. These are based on the assumption that the degree of liberalisation already reached by certain countries does not give them any real defence in a multilateral negotiation vis-à-vis those countries whose liberalisation process is much less advanced. Advocates of reciprocity argue that such countries have no real incentive to deeper liberalisation, given their benefits from the MFN system.

To present reciprocity as an alternative to MFN is a major departure from the trading system built up over 50 years, and it is just the opposite of what the founding fathers of the multilateral system envisaged. A nation or regional group which believes itself to be an open market has the right to fight hard to obtain from all its partners the greatest possible degree of liberalisation. If this argument is used tactically and temporarily as a negotiating device, there is less need for alarm over its implications for the system as a whole. But if alarm over its implications for the system as a whole. But if it becomes a permanent instrument of policy, then the risk for the multilateral system could become serious.

Trade is technical in its substance but highly political in its consequences. Reciprocity as a structural alternative to the multilateral system equals bilateralism; bilateralism equals discrimination; and trade relations based on power rather than rules are the result. This would be a very dangerous departure from the success story of the multilateral system.

The *growth of regionalism* is a more complex issue. There is no natural contradiction between regionalism and the multilateral system. This has been the shared assessment of the great majority of the international trade community. The real contradiction, it must always be emphasised, is between open trade and protectionism. Regional trade initiatives can certainly help to lower trade barriers and thus promote economic growth. But the relationship between regionalism and a multilateral system based on the MFN principle is nonetheless a complex one. The provisions of the GATT have sought to ensure compatibility by requiring regional agreements to cover substantially all trade among the partners and to promoted trade policies which do no lead to higher protection or extra restrictions on the trade of non-members. In practice, however, it has been almost impossible to assess the consistency of regional agreements.

The relation between regional and multilateral liberalisation in practice has been a different and generally more positive story. For example, successive enlargements of the European Union have been followed by multilateral trade negotiations, which have maintained a *de facto* link between progress at the regional level and at the multilateral level. These links are the reason why most people have seen regional agreements as building blocks for multilateral free trade.

Until quite recently, there was only one large regional grouping, and that was limited to a number of western European countries. The US was historically opposed to regionalism. But this situation has changed since the 1980s, the US has begun to build its own regional agreements, through free trade with Canada, through NAFTA, and through APEC, etc. Now, almost all the member countries of the WTO also belong to a regional trade agreement. The importance of regional agreements as a means of tariff reduction has declined (this is also thanks to the success of the GATT). Regional agreements are becoming more and more important in terms of trade rules, and for the political weight they represent in international negotiations. These are elements, which could break up the parallelism between regional and multilateral progress; there is the risk that antagonism between regional groups could make progress in the multilateral system more difficult.

Furthermore, regional initiatives such as the suggestions for a trans-Atlantic free trade area could give the impression of re-erecting a discriminatory divide between the rich North and the poorer South. One must be very attentive to strengthening the linkage which has existed up to now between regional and multilateral progress. What this means in practical terms is that regional liberalisation initiatives must proceed almost in tandem with multilateral ones. What countries are willing to do regionally, they must then be willing to do multilaterally, so as to keep this parallelism between regional and multilateral commitments.

At the core of this relationship, there is the basic question of the kind of international system, that is needed a global system based on the principle of non-discrimination embodied in agreed and enforceable rules, or a world divided into regional blocs with all the consequences this would imply for political stability and security.

An Unusual Historic Opportunity

To sum up, it is clear that the challenges facing the multilateral trading system are about much more than trade matters as they used to be defined. For some people—and for some countries too—the pace of change is unsettling and even alarming. Whether in the challenges that the information revolution presents to anyone over 30, or in the pace of economic globalisation, there is an understandable reflex which asks the world to slow down a little. However, we know it will not.

That is why there is a need to keep the multilateral system, with its reliable framework of principles and rules in good repair; it is a firm foothold in a shifting world. Liberalisation within the multilateral system means that this unstoppable process can be implemented within internationally agreed rules and disciplines. This is the opposite of a chaotic and unchecked process—without the security of the multilateral system, change would indeed be a leap in the dark.

At the same time, the multilateral system is becoming more and more a political issue. This is happening because its evolution increasingly concerns national regulatory policies more than cross-border obstacles, and it is happening because the challenges to the system are increasingly political rather than technical. In this context, it could become very important to consider the possibility of strengthening the institutional basis of the system, for example by enhancing the political dimension of its central institution, the WTO.

The confluence of political and economic events of the last few years places everyone on the threshold of an unusual historic opportunity: that of establishing a truly global system for the conduct of international economic relations, a system that responds readily to change and to changing needs, and one for which every nation will wish to claim ownership.

26

Beyond the Uruguay Round

Opportunities and Challenges

The successful conclusion of the Uruguay Round was the most significant economic event of 1994. The Round contributed to liberalisation of trade in goods, services and investment. It represents a decisive step towards introducing market solutions in international transactions. It entails significant potential gains for the world economy. But the distribution of gains across regions, nations and various groups within countries will be uneven, giving rise to certain challenges and risks. These merit the attention of the international community.

The process of trade liberalisation intensifies the trend towards globalisation. Free movements of goods and services across countries will mean greater mobility of capital and foreign direct investment. These factors taken together should contribute to the efficiency of the world economy by encouraging countries to produce goods and services in which they hold a comparative advantage. International competition on price and quality will thus intensify, leading to the development of new products and processes.

The downside of this process is, however, that it can accelerate two other trends. The first is the concentration of market structures, both at the global and national levels. The role of transnational corporations in the world economy is increasing, and while much stress is justifiably laid on promoting small and medium sized enterprises, there is no doubt that big business will have a growing role in economic activities not only in developed but also in developing countries. Even if measures are taken to prevent, through competition policy, possible abuses of dominant positions by large enterprises, the trend towards concentration of market power through globalisation will continue to have important implications for world trade and production.

The second trend is towards the potential marginalisation of poor nations and vulnerable groups within nations. The least developed countries, particularly in sub-Saharan Africa, for example, will experience losses in the short and even medium term as a result of the Uruguay Round agreements. They lack sufficient supply capacity to produce and export goods for which market access has improved. More importantly, they will not be able to exercise policy options that were available to the newly industrialized countries during their early development stage. Further, their competitive position in the world economy might be weakened with the new trends towards regionalism, as well as new methods of production.

Conversely, the intensification of international competition will inevitably enhance the position of the most efficient producers, with implications for the location of industries, and hence for employment. This will add fuel to the arguments of the advocates of protectionism.

Therefore, although the world economy as a whole benefits from trade liberalisation, there are risks of marginalisation which may lead to tensions among nations and among various groups within them and eventually could result in trade conflicts, undermining the security of the international trading system. The threat of instability of the trading system arises, in a sense, from a sort of "prisoners dilemma" whereby the common interests of the universe as a whole may diverge from the perceived individual interests of the main participating countries. Countries have a common interest in liberalizing international trade. However, individual countries may feel their interest lies in restricting trade so as to, inter alia, "protect" jobs. The balance could then be tipped in favour of protectionism, either overt or disguised as anti-dumping measures or environmental criteria and health and labour standards applied unilaterally. Likewise, the argument for the protection of strategic industries may be invoked.

As the invisible hand of the market by itself is insufficient to bring about social justice at the national level, market forces alone are equally incapable of preserving the common interest of all nations in a globalized world economy. A liberalized global economy requires a suitable framework of governance and institutions. In particular, like the need for a social safety net at the national level to avert social conflicts, there is also a need for a safety net at the international level to prevent the weakening of the international trading system, the environmental commons and peaceful international relations. Our existing institutional set-ups tend to lag behind economic changes, both at the national and international levels.

At the national level there is need for strengthening the social mechanisms and to pay closer attention to the distributional aspects of the benefits of production and trade; this is also true at the international level. Furthermore, there is a need for strengthening the socio-economic functions in order to find pragmatic solutions to universal problems arising from change and to preserve the common interests of people everywhere. Sound analysis is called for in this regard. A creative approach is needed, departing as necessary from conventional views, and aimed at arriving at commitments implementable by all.

27

Developing Countries and the Uruguay Round

An Evaluation and Prospects for the Future

The Uruguay Round was the most ambitious trade negotiation in history. It covered a wide variety of subjects relating to trade in goods; it brought under the aegis of multilateral disciplines two new sectors—agriculture and textiles—which had previously been exempt from such disciplines; it established new rules for services and intellectual property; and it set up a new World Trade Organisation (WTO) charged with supervising the results of the Round and continuing negotiations on all trade-related questions.

This article focuses on key issues of interest to developing countries. They are: (a) market access for developing country exports; (b) new restrictions on trade and industrial policy formulation in developing countries; (c) the effectiveness of the new safeguards and anti-dumping mechanisms in deterring protectionism; (d) the protection of intellectual property rights; (e) services; (f) the status of the principle of special and differential (S & D) treatment; and (g) institutional reforms and the creation of the WTO. An evaluation of the Round from the point of view of developing countries must necessarily attempt to weigh all of these elements.

The results of the Uruguay Round do not represent a good deal for developing countries. As regards improved market access for developing country exports, tariffs on products of interest to developing countries have been cut, but they will remain at higher levels than those applied to products traded mainly among developed countries; moreover, tariff escalation will be reduced but not significantly. The Round will bring about only marginal improvements in market access in the crucial areas of agriculture and textiles. Developing countries should continue to fight for the removal of tariffs on those goods that are of export interest to them and for the elimination of tariff escalation.

Market access will also depend on the abolition of grey area measures, their replacement by transparent and clearly temporary safeguard provisions, and the disciplining of antidumping practices. The new safeguards mechanism agreed to in the Round is due to replace grey area measures. However, the agreement legitimizes quantitative restrictions (QRS) directed at individual exporters, albeit with fairly stringent limitations as to duration and proof of injury procedures. Moreover, it remains to be seen in practice whether importers will resort to safeguards or will prefer the route of anti-dumping measures, which will remain easier to apply. Indeed, the anti-dumping agreement can be considered the major loophole of the Final Act and may well lead to a recrudescence of protectionism in both developed and—by imitation—developing countries.

The single most important achievement of the Uruguay Round was the setting up, under the aegis of the WTO, of an integrated and strengthened dispute settlement mechanism. While cross retaliation has been legitimised as a last resort, defendants will no longer be able to veto panel decisions that go against them. However, it is not yet clear to what extent the new dispute settlement mechanism will succeed in deterring major importers from having recourse to unilateral measures (such as those taken by the United States under the cover of Section 301 of its 1984 Trade Act).

As a result of the Round, there has been a significant upward harmonisation of trade and industrialisation policy disciplines towards the standards prevailing in developed countries. Henceforth, developing countries will face considerably more stringent restrictions in these areas, and their access to foreign technology will become more uncertain and costly. The Round has also resulted in a significant erosion in the international consensus in favour of special and differential (S & D) treatment for developing countries in the international trading system.

As the accords are implemented, developing countries will experience balance-of-payments difficulties. There will be a need to provide developing countries with greater International Monetary Fund (IMF) financing during the transition to the new disciplines, many of which will have adverse repercussions on the balance of payments of developing countries. Some of the agreements with balance-of-payments implications for developing countries are the adoption and enforcement of stricter intellectual property legislation, the agreement on agriculture, and the restrictions on the use of trade measures to protect the balance of payments.

The Final Act calls for cooperation between the WTO, the World Bank and the IMF. In the long-term, the main area of cooperation ought to be ensuring the consistency of international policies in the areas of trade, money and finance in order to ensure high rates of growth in the world economy and in developing countries in particular. It is especially important that such cooperation does not become an additional source of pressure on developing countries or restrict their degree of freedom in policy formulation and implementation.

In future trade negotiations, developing countries should emphasize improvements in the S & D principle, which should be made contractual in all of its dimensions. As a *quid pro quo,* developing countries should be ready to accept internationally agreed and binding criteria for graduation from the special and differential treatment category. Thus, belonging to the category of "developing" would no longer be a matter of self-election. Likewise, developed countries would no longer be able to graduate countries at their own discretion. Countries classified as developing would enjoy access to a truly generalised and universal GSP and temporary derogation from some of the disciplines imposed on developed countries. These derogations would apply to all areas of the agreement. The criteria used for graduation ought to include, besides per capita GDP, indicators of the level of industrial development. In the short term, the S & D principle can be usefully applied, in the process of "tariffication" of NTBs called for in the agreement on agriculture, by giving developing countries access to developed country markets at lower bound tariff rates than those applicable to developed country exporters.

The agreement on safeguards has problematic aspects. Close monitoring will be required so as to prevent the major trading partners—and, perhaps, by imitation, some developing countries themselves—from using the loopholes in the agreement (particularly the right to use QRs and the "quota modulation" provision) to reintroduce grey area measures, now under the legal cover of the safeguards agreement. The addition of a clause calling for payment of financial compensation to parties affected by quantitative safeguards when they exceed a certain maximum duration would deter countries from abusing the system. To be sure, the Uruguay Round cannot be considered to have settled the debate on this issue.

The Uruguay Round has given legal sanction to the new protectionism in the form of very unsatisfactory anti-dumping rules. This is an area that will undoubtedly continue to figure prominently on the agenda of future international trade negotiations. As a minimum, all the facts presented to national panels in anti-dumping cases should be subject to review by the Dispute Settlement Board. The use of reconstructed values in determining the existence of dumping and calculating dumping margins should be eliminated altogether. The anti-dumping mechanism would be improved if a clear distinction were made between price discrimination (which ought to be legal) and predatory pricing. The optimal solution would be to eliminate anti-dumping completely and to include the issue of predatory pricing within the framework of competition policy.

Harmonisation of competition policy has often been mentioned as a major item for the post-Uruguay Round trade agenda. Two issues of particular interest to developing countries in this area relate to investment measures and intellectual property. Particular TRIMs—such as export performance, local content, and trade-balancing requirements were seen in the Uruguay Round mainly as trade distortions, although they are also means of offsetting the restrictive business practices of transnational corporations. These practices should be subsumed under efforts to harmonize international competition policies. Similarly, many intellectual property issues impinge directly on competition policy. Impediments to "parallel" imports of patented goods can give rise to questions of competition. A major competition policy issue is the question of the scope and length of patent protection.

Much remains to be done in the area of trade in services. Developing countries ought to press for greater liberalisation of the temporary movement of skilled labour and labour working in the employment of services companies. The initial offers on services in the framework of the General Agreement on Trade in Services (GATS) largely exclude this code of delivery of services to foreign markets, a mode of critical interest to developing countries. Great caution and selectivity needs to be exercised with regard to the liberalisation of financial services; in this respect, the GATS gives developing countries the legal instrument to follow a gradual and selective approach. However, they will have to be prepared to resist bilateral pressures from some of their developed country partners to liberalize their financial services sector too rapidly.

Incorporation into the WTO implies a major domestic challenge for most developing countries. They will have to make efforts to change and adapt domestic legislation in a large number of new areas, including services, intellectual property, and several areas of trade policy that have received little attention in the past (e.g. safeguards, subsidies, and anti-dumping). The enforcement and administrative capacities of national institutions will have to be built up.

The WTO has been given a mandate to include in future negotiations any trade-related subject. The issues of environment and labour standards seem to be first in line. It will not be an easy matter to harmonize policies in these areas.

The reason is that harmonisation can be expected to take the form of aligning policies on developed country standards. It would be naive to pretend that the demands of environmental groups and labour unions on these matters can simply be ignored. Therefore, the challenge ahead is to participate constructively in drafting multilateral rules which expand or preserve access to markets and preclude punitive unilateral action, while taking into consideration environmental and labour concerns.

28

Developing Countries and the WTO Agricultural Negotiations

Developing countries as a group have much to gain from continued progress toward a transparent, rule-based trading system in agriculture. The researchers say the negotiations should eliminate export subsidies, impose stricter disciplines on export taxes, cut tariffs, and ensure that food aid continues to be available to poor countries in grant form and delivered so as not to displace domestic production in the countries receiving it. Badly managed food aid, or cheap food imports due to export subsidies, may just reinforce the bias of economic policies against the rural sector. With its negative impact on poor agricultural producers, they say. International research organisations (such as IFPRI, among other institutions) may provide support to developing countries through programmes of collaborative research, technical assistance, and capacity strengthening.

Starting with the first round of trade negotiations under the General Agreement on Tariffs and Trade (GATT) after World War II, there has been a relatively steady trend of increasing multilateral trade liberalisation. The successive rounds of negotiations recognised the greater needs of developing countries, especially since the Tokyo Round. Yet the participation of developing countries was limited. Since many developing countries were not members of GATT, the major forum for airing their views was provided by the United Nations Conference on Trade and Development. The views of developing countries had some impact on the Lome agreements and on aid flows, but had limited influence on negotiations concerning trading rules, which were discussed within the framework of the GATT, where OECD (Organisation for Economic Cooperation and Development) countries set the agenda.

In the Uruguay Round, which began in 1986 and concluded in 1993, developing countries played a larger role in the negotiations compared to previous rounds. In particular, agricultural net exporters organised the Cairns Group (which in addition to Australia, New Zealand and Canada, included several large developing countries such as Argentina, Brazil, Indonesia, and the Philippines) to pursue their interests. Furthermore, during and after the conclusion of the Uruguay Round, the formal accession of developing countries to the GATT and now the World Trade Organisation (WTO) has continued apace. Of the 134 members of the WTO in February 1999, some 70 per cent were developing countries. The United Nations classified 48 countries as least-developed (LLDCs). Within that group, 29 are members of the WTO, six are in the process of accession, and three are observers. Also, 18 countries have been identified as net-food-importing developing countries (NFIDCs).

Some Definitions

The LLDCs are identified by the United Nations General Assembly based on several criteria—income per capita, augmented physical quality of life index, and an index of economic diversification. As a group, they have a population of about 590 million people, with an income per capita about 4 per cent that of the world average (1996). Agricultural production per capita in LLDCs has been declining since the 1970s although the same indicator for all developing countries (mainly under the influence of China) has gone up by nearly 40 per cent in the same period. LLDCs represent a small fraction of world trade (less than one per cent for total and about two per cent for agricultural trade). They had a positive, although declining net agricultural trade balance until the mid-1980s, when it turned negative. Almost 20 per cent of their total imports are food items.

The 18 net-food-importing developing countries have been selected through a process within the WTO. They have a population of some 380 million people and an income per capita nearly five times that of the LLDC average, but still much lower than the world average. NFIDCs are a diverse group: four are upper-middle income countries; eight are lower-middle income; and six are lower income. Four of them had net food exports on average during 1995-97, but because they imported cereals they are included in the group. NFIDCs' per capita food production as share of both world and developing country averages has risen, although from very low levels.

Although the categories of "developed" and "developing" countries have important legal consequences under WTO rules, there are no formal definitions of either category. The process works through self-identification and negotiation with other member countries of the WTO.

Completing the Unfinished Agenda

In general, developing countries operate under what has been called "special and differential treatment". They face lower disciplines and enjoy longer timeframes for implementing reforms. In the case of LLDCs, they are totally exempted from WTO commitments, and it has been agreed that developing and least-developed countries should receive special consideration for market access and technical and financial support. Also, during the Uruguay Round, concerns that liberalisation of agricultural policies and trade could adversely affect the food imports of LLDCs and NFIDCs led participants to include several measures dealing with food security issues in the "green box" of permitted domestic support, for instance, the formation of public stockholding and the provision of foodstuffs at subsidised prices. There was a ministerial decision in Marrakesh in April 1994 to deal with possible negative effects of agricultural trade reforms on the food security of LLDCs and NFIDCs. The decision was reemphasised at the 1996 ministerial meeting of the WTO in Singapore.

Export and Domestic Subsidies

While many developing countries have significantly reduced distorting domestic agricultural policies, the possible benefits that these countries and the world can enjoy are thwarted by the subsidies of developed countries. The Uruguay Round was a first step in imposing discipline on the unfair competition arising from subsidised agricultural exports, which hurts poor agricultural producers in developing countries irrespective of their net agricultural trade position. In the next negotiations, that first step should be completed with the elimination of export subsidies. Net-food-importing developing countries should also be interested in stricter disciplines on export taxes and controls that exacerbate price fluctuations in world markets.

Under the Uruguay Round agreement, there is still a lot of scope for the developed countries to use domestic subsidies, in addition to the use of export subsidies; to help their farmers. The developing countries should seek further disciplines in this regard, including, among other things, the elimination of exemptions under the "blue box" (which allows farmers to receive some forms of direct payments that are considered to be trade distorting). Least-developed and developing countries, however, will still be allowed "special and differential treatment" on these issues.

Market Access

If the developing countries are to succeed in diversifying their agricultural sectors, they need expanded access to markets in developed countries. This includes increasing the volume of imports allowed under the current regime of tariff-rate quotas (TRQs, which replaced the previous system of rigid quotas with a combination of a quantitative quota and a high tariff for the eventual out-of-quota imports); making the administration of the TRQs more transparent and equitable; seeking further reductions in tariffs, particularly those still high in some key products; and completing the process of tariffication in the cases where exemptions were granted. Also, eliminating, or at least reducing, tariffs escalation in non-agricultural products is important for developing countries: this practice undermines the possibilities of expanding production and exports of processed goods that use agricultural inputs, exploiting "forward linkages" in the value-added chain.

What the Most Vulnerable Need

The special situation and concerns of least-developed countries and net-food-importing countries were recognised in a ministerial decision agreed upon at the completion of the Uruguay Round in 1993. These concerns include the preservation of adequate levels of food aid, the provision of technical assistance and financial support to develop the agricultural sector in those countries, and the continuation and expansion of financial facilities to help with structural adjustment and short-term difficulties in financing food imports. It is important to make food aid available in grant form, to target it to poor countries and social groups, and to deliver it in ways that do not displace domestic production in the countries receiving it. Badly managed food aid, or cheap food imports due to export subsidies, may just reinforce the bias of economic policies against the rural sector, with its negative impact on poor agricultural producers.

Volatility in agricultural prices must be monitored carefully. While expansion of world agricultural trade should limit overall fluctuations by spreading supply and demand shocks over larger areas, the decline in world public stocks as a percentage of consumption works in the opposite direction. Improving early warning of potential food shortages, lowering costs for food transportation and storage, and providing better targeted food aid programmes and financial facilities for emergencies are also issues that need to be addressed by countries participating in the coming round of negotiations.

The impact of changes in trade and agricultural policy on poorer consumers and producers in developing countries is a matter of debate. Some have argued that trade liberalisation may hurt both groups. Others have answered that greater productivity and growth coming from better trade and sectoral policies should help generate employment and income, given a setting of adequate overall economic policies and properly functioning markets and social institutions.

Small producers will also be helped by the disciplines that the URAA is bringing subsidised and dumped exports, while it allows the implementation of a variety of programmes aimed at poor producers or consumers, including stocks for food security purposes and domestic food aid for populations in need. The issue here is the adequate design and funding of domestic policies to achieve the intended objectives of agricultural growth and poverty alleviation, which most certainly will not be helped by trade-distorting interventions either in developed or developing countries.

In general, low-income developing countries and LLDCs should emphasise to the international community the importance of creating and expanding a supportive international trade and financial environment and of implementing an integrated framework for economic and social development, with agricultural and trade polices being an integral part of the strategy. Appropriate measures would include—in addition to the agricultural trade issues suggested here—the continuation and enhancement of the reduction of the external debt of Heavily Indebted Poor Countries (the HIPC initiative) and the further liberalisation of trade in textiles.

But improved international conditions should go hand-in-hand with a better domestic framework in developing and least-developed countries, including stable macro-economic policies, open and effective markets, good governance, the rule of law, a vibrant civil society, and programmes and investments that expand opportunities for all, with special consideration for poor and disadvantaged groups.

Bringing Developing Countries into the Process

Developing countries, as small players in the global arena, should be interested and active participants in the design and implementation of international rules that limit the ability of larger countries to resort to unilateral action. Also, domestic legal and institutional frameworks in developing countries may be strengthened by the implementation of internationally negotiated rules that limit the scope for rent seeking and arbitrary projectionist measures. The developing countries as a group have much to gain from continued progress toward a transparent, rule-based, trading system in agriculture.

What are the requirements and skills for the developing countries to become effective members in the next WTO round? Any negotiation requires careful consideration of the legal, economic, and political dimensions that define the substance and possible evolution of the negotiations, as well as the diplomatic and negotiating techniques that may help in the attainment of the expected outcomes. Questions that need to be addressed include:

- What are the economic and social consequences of different WTO scenarios (quantitative estimation of impacts)? Knowing the impacts of alternative scenarios is crucial if developing countries are to represent their interests in the negotiation process.
- What are the legal issues being discussed (definition of obligations, exemptions, timeframe, and so on)? Detailed knowledge of international trade law is crucial if developing countries are not to be "shortchanged." The devil is in the details.
- Looking at the political process, who are the main actors and their interests and what type of alliances may drive the negotiations? Negotiators must understand the political economy of their own country

and of other countries in the WTO if they are to negotiate effectively.

- With these elements, an adequate diplomatic and negotiating strategy must be defined and implemented.

Developing countries that have carefully considered all four components will be better prepared to participate effectively in the coming negotiations. Of course, limited financial and human resources act as an important constraint. However, developing countries may overcome some of the problems through collective action, for instance considering the creation of alliances with respect to their main export and import commodities and the markets they approach for their exports. An example is the Cairns Group. This approach could reduce the fixed costs of negotiations. Spreading them over groups of countries, allow a better use of scarce technical expertise, and improve the bargaining position of developing countries. It could also be in the interest of the OECD countries to deal with negotiating blocs, which represent a smaller number of negotiating positions, rather than with numerous separate countries. The negotiations would be much more efficient and balanced.

29

Trading Towards Peace

The reason why trade has such a vital part to play in building peace is because it means lowering barriers—not only to goods and services but among nations and peoples. The elimination of barriers creates interdependence and interdependence creates solidarity. The history of the last fifty years has shown us all the undeniable benefits of lowering trade barriers and opening economies.

Clearly every region has its own characteristics, and it would be wrong to imagine that the same blueprint can apply everywhere and in the same way. Any region which was for thousands of years at the crossroads of world trade should regain its place in the centre, because doing so will help build peace as well as prosperity. This is why the numerous applications for accession to the WTO from various countries are so significant. The first is through regionalism. There are several efforts at regional trade and economic initiatives among countries, and that such initiatives will be encouraged to reduce positive results. Regional initiatives are important because they can help countries at a comparable level of development to move relatively quickly in opening their economies and in deepening their interdependence.

However, the rapid advance of global economic integration means that while regional initiatives remain important, they are not sufficient by themselves to address successfully the new perspectives of the international economy. That is why there is a need for second track, which is the rule-based multilateral system, and that is why the multilateral system is of fundamental importance to the economic prosperity of any region.

As the first major international institution to be created in the post-Cold War era, the WTO offers a promise of the kind of global economic architecture which need in the coming decades. Its culture is firmly rooted in the tradition of consensus-building and cooperation among sovereign countries. And the WTO embodies rights and obligations negotiated by consensus, approved and ratified by each government and each parliament, and they are enforceable, not through the crude exercise of economic power, but through the rule of law. The alternative would be a power-based system—who would want to chose this option?

But most importantly, the WTO is an organisation which brings all countries—from all corners of the world and from all levels of development—together as equals. There is no weighted voting, no exclusive clubs, no inner and outer circles. Developing countries representing 80 per cent of constituency sit as equals with industrialised countries to write the rules of a shared trading system.

This new unity of developing and developed countries inside a single system will be credited as the greatest achievement of the multilateral system. But this unity is still fragile: we cannot allow it to be broken: This is why, in preparing the agenda of the first Ministerial meeting in Singapore, have recognised the particularly difficult task facing developing countries in implementing the Uruguay Round Commitments. They have also acknowledged the challenges they face in contemplating the necessary work programme.

The integration of developing countries as equal partners in the multilateral system is one of the most important challenges in shaping the economic order of the 21st century. This is a shared responsibility of developed and developing countries alike. There is no rational alternative to this objective. The evolution of the global economy makes that clear.

Now there is a need to work together as equal partners to ensure the full integration, and all other developing and transition economies, into the global economy and the rule-based multilateral trading system. In conjunction with this there is a need to encourage, notably with growth of regional economic cooperation. The alternative is a vicious circle where economic isolation feeds greater political instability which in turn leads to greater economic isolation. The road to a lasting peace in the world begins, not ends, with economic integration and interdependence. Taking this message to heart will help build a future where its goods, services, and investment that cross borders—not missiles and soldiers.

30

The Role of Financial Markets and the IMF

The Genesis of Asia's Financial Crisis

It is obvious that the major causes of Asia's financial crisis were rooted in the affected countries. The evils were excessive foreign borrowing, poor supervision of banks, and overvaluation of national currencies. Apart from those policy failures, however, there were external factors. These were, besides the instability of the international finance markets, above all the wrong reaction of the International Monetary Fund, which aggravated the crisis rather than counteracting it. The role of the IMF must be fundamentally redefined.

The Asian crisis marks for the time being the end of the Southeast and East Asian economic miracle of the last four decades. Engulfed by the malaise of the worst-hit countries, Thailand, Indonesia and South Korea, the entire region is suffering economic weakness and in part even a decline in economic performance. The question is whether the Asian crisis could have been avoided or whether wrong economic policy decisions gave it a kick-start.

The Causes of the Crisis

Analysis of the causes for the Asian crisis have to date been marked by an astonishing one-sidedness. Up front, explanations emphasise the internal causes, particularly the private sector's excessive foreign borrowing. But two other factors played central, if not decisive, roles in the spread of the crisis. One was the great volatility of the international capital markets, the other the inappropriate policies of the IMF.

This article analysis these three major causes of the crisis. Another question is how in future one can prevent manageable economic problems getting out of hand and developing into a crisis that threatens more than the economic stability of single countries.

But a closer look shows that the crisis, which broke out in mid-1997, has assumed such an unforeseen dimension that individual corrective measures of economic policy can no longer cope with it. A huge structural economic crisis has arisen. What developments led to it ?

Foreign Borrowing

Let us look first at the high private sector borrowing abroad. With hindsight, it is easy to pass judgement on it as having been wrong and dangerous. But that does not mean that private foreign borrowing is harmful in general. If it finances profitable investments, it is merely the use of foreign savings when domestic savings are too low. IMF reports also reflected this assessment.

We know from experience of earlier debt crisis that a high foreign indebtedness by the private sector is latently, but not generally, risky. The Asian crisis also has reconfirmed that international finance markets differentiate between individual private debtors and the credit-worthiness of national economies only in the case of a few countries. In smaller countries, including OECD member South Korea, difficulties in servicing individual loans lead to investors getting out of these markets. This is the real danger of large-scale private foreign debts.

That makes foreign loans much more expensive than domestic credits. If the national interest rate is higher than that of international market, cash deposit requirement often can be an adequate incentive to borrow at home or take out a longer-term loan. Both alternatives lead to greater stability of the domestic finance system, as the risk of withdrawal of capital at short notice, as in the case of the Asian crisis countries, is much reduced.

Instability of the Finance Markets

Beyond the cash deposit requirement, however, further restructuring must be done in the finance sectors of the Asian crisis economies and threshold and developing countries. Frequently, there are demands for greater transparency. Improved banking supervision and, especially in the case of South Korea, a broader diversification of shareholding. These steps are important, but they will not prevent the next crisis because they do not put an end to the instability of the international finance markets.

The Asian crisis has also reconfirmed that highly mobile capital can produce instability. It must seem dubious when there are calls (particularly by the IMF and US politicians involved in financial matters) for the pushing through of even more capital mobility as a consequence of the crisis. But even liberal economists are now increasingly questioning the ideal of a world without restrictions on the free movement of capital linked with an enhanced IMF mandate.

IMF Intervention

The IMF's policy intensified the volatility of the international capital flows, that is, their wide fluctuation margin. When American and European fund managers began to pull their capital out of Asia's crisis countries. Asian debtors fell into arrears in servicing their liabilities, and the currencies came under heavy pressure, the IMF ordered a drastic cure. This was aimed at lowering inflation rates and reducing government budget deficits. But as there were no critical inflation rates, and government budgets were, in fact, in surplus, this policy was more than odd. A quick look at the economic development in the Asian crisis countries illustrates the relatively positive situation of the three economies before the crisis broke out.

What Measures to Stabilise Currencies?

The IMF policy also manifests deficiencies beyond the measures it ordered. I shall not discuss here the question of whether it is wise and appropriate for the IMF to clamp measures and restrictions of private sector debtors and their governments while the creditors side can emerge from the crisis largely without loss.

But one must ask whether the IMF's measures to stabilise the currencies were suitable in an acute-crisis. They are mainly measures with individual impacts, giving priority to increasing real interest rates. The aim is to regain the trust of international finance markets and stimulate fresh loan flows to these countries. The long-term objective is to restore currency stability.

This policy, however, has two weaknesses. On the one hand, it sets indebted companies under more pressure as they must not only pay more for their foreign currency loans due to devaluation, but are also faced with higher domestic interest. On the other hand, while it is true that a high interest rate policy in countries with stable economies can have a positive impact in attracting capital, that is not so in countries suffering from an acute economic crisis, as Indonesia shows. Recovery of the exchange rate to a realistic level that would enable the companies to service their debts has not happened there.

The Future of the IMF

Having reflected upon the dubious results of the IMF policy, one is bound to ask what role the organisation should play in future. Should its task be to have a stabilising effect in a crisis, or should the IMF be an instrument to assert certain economic policy concepts?

The IMF itself has defined its current function very one-sidedly, focusing on its services for the international finance markets. According to a self-assessment in an internal IMF document, it sees itself performing a dual function as a 'confidental economic adviser' and as the 'watchdog for the international financial markets'. But the IMF does not by a long way give the attention they deserve to the interests of the 350 million people in the countries under its wing.

Criticism in the West

Criticism of the IMF is growing not only in the Asian crisis countries but also especially in the USA and more and more in Europe. Conservative American politicians such as the former US Secretary of State Charles Shultz, have described the IMF as ineffective, unnecessary and obsolute. They have also proposed that the IMF be abolished at some time after the Asian crisis has been overcome. The IMF's current policy is also coming in for heavy criticism in the academic debate on the crisis, which is demanding a redefinition of the organisation's mandate.

Other possibilities are conceivable beyond the radical option of abolishing or privatising the IMF. The IMF should in any case be required to tackle the specific situations in the crisis countries with greater awareness of the affected countries. In the course of the Asian crisis, the option of creating a regional fund was also discussed, but the Western G7 countries and the IMF emphatically rejected it. One should, however, consider whether regional institutions could not, in fact, work more efficiently than an authority based in Washington with competence for the entire world.

A regional structure with several monetary funds could facilitate the overcoming of crisis situations, although only if a global structure were to be maintained alongside the regional components. This global body, a kind of world monetary council, would be composed of representatives of the US and European central banks and the regional funds. Besides taking over the IMF's current tasks, such an international regime could also deal with stabilising exchange rates between the industrialised nations and in particular with the development of a target zones system between the dollar and the Euro. The winners in a less unstable international finance system would be the developing and threshold countries that at present still need to take the questionable medicine prescribed by the IMF.

31

Richer or Poorer?

Achievements and Challenges of Ethical Trade

Ethical trade as an approach to supply chain management has mushroomed in recent years. Northern companies are becoming increasingly concerned with the 'ethics' of their operations and the risks to reputation and productivity posed by bad employment practices in global supply chains. But can voluntary private sector codes really improve employment conditions in supply chains?

Ethical trade is one dimension of corporate social responsibility, bringing social issues into the mainstream of commercial supply chain management through the use of codes of conduct. It is sometimes confused with fair-trade which addresses terms of trading for smaller producers, and fosters greater responsibility in supply chain relations.

Ethical trade, on the other hand, focuses on workplace issues, requiring that supplier's in particular meet minimum employment, worker welfare and aspects of human rights standards.

Similar management systems are well established for product safety and environmental issues. Here, we focus on the social dimensions of ethical trade and its codes of conduct yet the separation of social and environmental standards is increasingly artificial in global sourcing agreements. A plethora of codes are on offer. The most numerous are in-houses codes such as Nike's 233 company codes counted in 1999 and the figure is rising.

Suppliers have to comply with and pay for a multitude of similar but different codes. Harmonising codes or establishing equivalence is on the agenda but has not yet halted the problem of 'code overload'.

At a broader level, industry-specific codes have also been developed. The US Apparel industry Partnership/Fair Labour Agreement adopted by a number of leading US merchandising companies is a good example. Industry standards are not new, as ISO and EMAS environmental management systems show. Building on ISO principles, Social Accountability International (formerly CEPAA) has development SA8000. This is an independent social standard that can be used as an auditable code throughout the private sector.

Ethical trade is partly a response to consumer and campaigning group pressure in globalised economy. Alliances of companies, NGOs, trade. Developing codes of conduct through a multi-stakeholder approach is a striking aspect of ethical trade, bringing together companies, NGOs, trade unions and some government departments. An example of this collaborative approach is the Ethical Trading Initiative (ETI) in the UK. The ETI's baseline code of conduct that corporate members from various industries must comply with as a minimum standard is more than just a code, ETI aims to provide a learning environment and sponsors pilot projects in developing countries to test different methods of monitoring and verification.

Codes of conduct need to be assessed in terms of content, implantation and impact. A number of professional auditing companies have moved into this area, some accredited to audit specific codes such as FLA or SA8000. Suppliers audited against a specific code undergo an inspection, and where non-compliance is found, have to take remedial action or risk failing the audit.

Social auditing is a complex process, however, and it can be difficult to spot workplace abuse, such as sexual harassment or forced overtime. Workers have little confidence in a process that appears to be linked with management, and fear that reporting issues could risk their jobs. Advocates of the multi-stakeholder approach argue that effective monitoring and verification of codes must involve local NGOs and trade unions in which workers have trust. Participatory social auditing, also a means of raising awareness and of facilitating behavioural change, can help reveal serious management problems. But in many developing countries local organisations lack the capacity to participate: developing sustainable local systems of monitoring and verification remains an important challenge.

Do the advantages of multi-stakeholder approaches outweigh immediate constraints? Ethical trade is a largely northern driven process, reflecting Western ethical thinking and priorities. Southern based initiatives, however, are expanding, raising the possibility of local ownership of codes. Collaboration poses challenges. Stronger relationships and better understanding are essential between southern and northern workers, producers, trade unions, and NGOs for codes to work globally.

But there is still scepticism as to the extent of the benefits that ethical trade might bring. Will increasing southern capacity to participate, as the ETI has done in its pilot project, help? Will building trust, confidence and dialogue achieve the objectives of ethical trade, north and south? Child labour is often more complex, however, than codes make it appear. Codes meet to address the conditions of all workers within the supply chain, including the least visible; partnerships must include all groups to address these limitations.

The role of government is hotly contested. Can a system whose credibility depends on under-resourced civil society actors, often excluding democratically elected representatives, maintain genuine credibility? If the boundaries between private sector and public sector roles are not defined, the list of private sector responsibilities will become unmanageable. Private sector initiatives are not a substitute for more comprehensive national or international development policies.

What are the consequences of codes? Do they encourage downsizing or reinforce from large suppliers where compliance is more easily monitored? There is a risk that the gains of some will be at the expense of others.

Ethical trade has successfully begun forging partnerships to find solutions. While it might be wrong to assume that ethical trade can change the world, handled wisely it could make a world of difference for some. Yet it is not a panacea for development. Issues that remain unchallenged by ethical trade include:

- The exclusion of companies producing for domestic markets—often bigger employers.
- Underlying causes of poverty and social marginalisation.

32

What's Driving Migration?

The scale and diversity of today's migrations are beyond any previous experience. Rapid urban growth and environmental degradation in rural areas have led to internal migration affecting hundreds of million of people. Migration is now seen as a priority issue equal in political weight to other major global challenges, such as the environment, population growth and economic imbalances between regions.

Families and households form the basis for economic growth, social development and personal fulfilment. Decisions, by individual women and men on marriage, family, a place to live, shape the destinies of communities and nations. National policies and international conditions provide the context for individual decision-making. Effective development policies, including population, reproductive health and family planning policies, address this reality.

Data on national and global population trends set the agenda for national policy. An important element of population programmes is gathering data that will allow policy-making responsive to the realities of daily life, and to the needs and aspirations of individuals.

The dominant feature of global demographics is still growth. Age distribution is a growing concern, as the numbers of young and elderly people, grow, relative to the working-age population. The world is growing steadily more urban.

From being a sign of strength and dynamism in the national economy, the rate and scale of urban growth has become increasingly a cause for concern. The influx of migrants to the biggest cities may be weakening both urban and rural sectors.

International migration is small in extent compared with internal movements, but has a disproportionate impact. Both internal and international migration are driven by population growth, and by inequities between countries. Migration is one of the choices which shape people's lives and the destiny of nations. But it can also be a symptom of inequity and underdevelopment. Migrants are by definition the most vulnerable members of the host community. Their living and working conditions should be protected.

Open and frank exchange of information and views between host and sending countries is needed more than ever. The aim of the international community should be to protect the right to move, but to ensure that movement is voluntary and that it stimulates rather than holds back personal and national development. "The point of departure should be the human right to live and work where one pleases, so long as it does not infringe on other people's rights to do the same."

The Urban Transformation

The rural sector is declining in importance and its contribution to national economies. It is increasingly part of a unified economy based on the city. Contact with the urban areas is easier than ever and is encouraged by rural development.

Temporary and circular migration is giving way to more permanent settlement. The largest cities are under increasing strain, and residents are encountering increasing difficulties in improving or even maintaining living conditions. Nevertheless, migration continues, driven by a variety of forces both positive and negative. The choice to move can be part of a strategy for survival or personal development; but it is often enforced by external conditions.

The urban transformation is irreversible, but the rural sectors must also be strengthened to balance the developing economy. Attention to gender issues will be crucial in ensuring a successful transition. The forces driving internal and international migration have much in common. Demographic pressures are contributing to both. As the pressures encouraging migration increase, the options for migrants become more limited. This collision is contributing to the atmosphere of crisis surrounding both urban and international migration.

Costs and Benefits

Migration is the result of individual or family decisions. But it is also part of social process. In economic terms, migration is as much a global phenomenon as trade in commodities or manufactured goods. It is part of a broader pattern, and evidence of changing economic, social and cultural relationships.

But migration may be evidence of a different kind of relationship: the combination of poverty, rapid population growth and environmental damage is a powerful destabilizing factor driving urban growth and eventually international migration. On the recipient side, migration has usually been seen as evidence of a thriving economy: today's industrial states were built in part by migrant labour, skills and investment. In today's increasingly uncertain conditions, migration may be seen as a threat to the security and well-being of the local workforce and society at large.

The only effective means to reduce migration pressures over the long term are to slow population growth; to stimulate economic growth and job creation at home, and promote the development of the individual and the family as the basic economic and social unit.

A Question of Gender

It is often assumed that most migrants are men, in reality, women make up nearly half of the international migrant population. Gender differences in social and economic roles affect migration decision-making, household strategy, and the sex composition of labour migration. Attention to the gender dimension of migratory movements ought to be an important component in population and development planning.

Women frequently take the initiative in migration decisions, which may reflect limited opportunities in rural areas. Low status limits women's choices at home and may increase pressure to migrate, but it may also affect life in the host community. Opportunities may be limited by lack of education or skills, or by customer limitation on women's freedom of action outside the family or ethnic group. Paid employment for migrant women is usually in the lowest wage, least secure, and lowest status jobs, mostly in housework, child care and trade.

Most educated women end up in the same low-status, low-wage production and service jobs as unskilled female migrants. Men too, experience downward mobility, but the contrast in the decline in women's employment status is far greater. Despite these disadvantages women migrants have become significant economic actors. Their status may be improved by migration, but the advantages are not clear-cut. Women's status as migrants is affected by their vulnerability, and by their lack of reproductive freedom. To ensure improved status they will need both legal protection and essential services, including reproductive health services.

Refugees

Refugees in the 1990s are overwhelmingly in Asia, Africa and Latin America. Their numbers are large, about 17 million, and growing rapidly. A further 3.5 to 4 million were thought to be in "refugee-like situation", though estimates are probably extremely conservative, and an estimated 23 million people internally displaced.

It is important to recognize the common roots of refugee and other forms of mass movement of populations. At the same time, despite the difficulty of distinguishing between political and socio-economic causes of migration, there is a clear need to distinguish between refugees and other groups of migrants. Participation in international efforts of burden-sharing would ensure that most refugee problems would be dealt with in their regions of origin.

Conclusions and Policies

Migration highlights linkages and interdependencies within countries, with many implications for development agendas, including population programmes and development assistance.

Policies to regulate or moderate international migration have concentrated largely on urban growth. They have been only intermittently effective. The most successful have concentrated on stimulating rural development and the growth of alternative urban centres

Migration is also a personal or family decision, which is affected by external conditions such as poverty or environmental degradation, improving conditions of personal and family life can make a crucial difference in the decision to migrate, reducing dependence on migration as a strategy. Because migration is the result of personal and family decisions, it can be influenced by policies that improve the quality of life.

This offers the opportunity for policies emphasizing individual development, among them education, health (including reproductive health) and family planning. Such policies are particularly relevant to the strategies, must take into account gender differences in social and economic life and the differential effects of policies.

Migration decisions are about family security and long-term-life-chances, rather than simply the maximisation of income. They are ultimately strategies designed to look after the individual's and the household's needs, safeguard their security, and respond to their aspirations. If the goal is to reduce migration pressure through development it will be essential to increase the capacity but reduce the need to migrate. Long-term external support will be required to make such policies a reality, particularly in areas of rapid population growth and potential mass outward flows. Highly co-ordinated allocation of development assistance can help establish priorities and focus attention on basic needs. The challenge to both international donors and co-operating governments is to direct programme spending to the areas where it can be most effective.

33

Solving the Unemployment Problem by Looking Beyond the Job

If you had a job, you worked; if you didn't, you didn't. Having a job meant being employed by an organisation in a clearly-defined and stable occupational role, with duties, hours, rates of pay and promotion all more or less standardised. But the job—in that meaning of the word—is a social invention, and a fairly recent one.

The job—the kind that you had, or hoped to get—became a central fixture of life. Its importance was great because it served many needs: For managers and efficiency experts, job assignments were the key to assembly-line manufacturing. For union organizers, jobs protected the rights of workers. For political reformers, standardised civil service positions were the essence of good government. Jobs provided an identity to immigrants and recently-urbanised farm workers. They provided a sense of security for individuals and an organising principle for society.

Jobs functioned in so many ways that it is surprising how many organizations are now opting for other ways to define and manage work. The second job shift is underway. Its emergence can be seen in the increasing use of temporary and part-time workers and contracted-out services, the changing relationships between workers and management, the growing popularity of self-employment and small business. Indeed, "de-jobbing" is proceeding at such a pace that many economists, management experts and futurists are now talking freely about the end of the job. Bridges predicts that the job as we now know it will disappear entirely—replaced by new kinds of flexible work assignments in post-job organizations—and be remembered only as a quaint artefact of the industrial age.

One reason for the change in work is the economic rules of the survival game among organizations that employ workers. To stay successful in today's hi-tech consumer economy, businesses have had to re-model themselves into what some experts call "agile companies"—ones that are able to respond quickly to conditions in ever-changing, fragmenting, competitive markets.

The "knowledge worker", whose work involves not simply doing something, but also applying theoretical or analytical skills. Such workers are replacing the industrial labourer as the dominant part of the workforce—and their productive activities are likely to be organised and structured much differently from those of their assembly-line predecessors.

De-jobbing as a result of new technology or the emergence of a service economy is a phenomenon that gets a lot of attention these days; but it is not the whole story. At all levels of society, people are improvising livelihoods that do not fit the industrial-era model. Immigrants to the developed countries, often unable to find steady jobs, nevertheless find places in the new landscape by being mobile, flexible, resourceful and imaginative. They moonlight, work part-time, share jobs, start small businesses. Their lives are often extremely difficult, but they are also instructive to those of us who believe you either have a job or you're out of luck.

It is too early to evaluate the implications of this multifaceted transformation of work, or to dismiss it as simply good or bad. Nevertheless, one cannot deny that it is taking place, and will bring about dramatic social changes.

On the downside, the job shift is causing great hardships for many workers and their families. It poses serious challenges to policy-makers, political activists and labour leaders. The basic question appears to be whether the key to global employment-development strategy is to play "catch-up"—trying to bring millions of people around the world into jobs in industries and the public sector, or to play "leapfrog"—creating new forms of employment.

The proposal to generate more employment in agriculture, for example, is based on new demand for agricultural exports from developing countries. The policies designed to make the most of this opportunity include measures to upgrade technology, raise productivity, ensure the supply o. essential inputs, establish marketing and distribution channels, create links between agriculture and industry, and cater to export markets.

The issue of part-time work, another kind of employment that is seriously undervalued in the traditional industrial-era job mind-set. Part-time work may not offer much at this point to developing countries, where many people are under-employed and wages are low, but it can be of great help in more advanced economies. And it is likely to be a big part of the global work picture in the years ahead.

A certain agility may also be necessary in agriculture, particularly in countries that for many years have depended heavily on producing commodities such as sugar for export as a means of generating income and employment. As Northern laboratories develop non-agricultural substitutes for many of these commodities—and this is already beginning to happen—the bottom may fall out of "monoculture" economies, only economic, but will have long-run political implications as communities attempt to reorganize themselves in response to the changed conditions. It is, therefore, in the interest of raw materials exporters to closely monitor current trends in biotechnology and the use of genetic resources and modify their internal policies in anticipation of potential long-term effects."

This calls for flexibility, and an ability to get information and to act on it. Government officials, development workers, community leaders and individuals will, in some respects, all have to be "knowledge workers" if they are to keep ahead of global changes. Jobs are going to be created not just by putting people to work, but by finding—or creating new niches where they can be productive.

It is still possible to talk about jobs for all, and to resist the assumption made by many economists that high levels of unemployment are now inevitable. But, as we move ahead into the global information economy, we may be moving back into an older conception of the job, and seeing it again as something you do, rather than as something you have—or that has you.

34

The Population Challenge

During the last half-century world population has more than doubled, climbing from 2.5 billion in 1950 to 5.9 billion in 1998. Those of us born before 1950 are members of the first generation to witness a doubling of world population. Stated otherwise, there has been more growth in pollution since 1950 than during the 4 million years since our early ancestors first stood upright.

This unprecedented surge in population combined with rising individual consumption, is pushing our claims on the planet beyond its natural limits. Water tables area falling on every continent as demand exceeds the sustainable yield of aquifers. Eventual aquifer depletion will bring irrigation cutbacks and shrinking harvests. Our growing appetite for seafood has pushed oceanic fisheries to their limits and beyond. Collapsing fisheries tell us we can go no further. The Earth's temperature is rising, promising changes in climate that we cannot even anticipate. We are triggering the greatest extinction of plant and animal species since the dinosaurs disappeared. As our numbers go up, their numbers go down.

These effects of population growth are relatively recent, but assertions that population growth could affect human welfare are not. In 1798 Thomas Malthus, a British clergyman and intellectual, warned in his famous piece, *An Essay on the Principles of Population*, of the tendency for population to grow exponentially while food supply grew arithmetically. He saw a world where human numbers would continually press against available food supplies.

During the 200 years since Malthus issued his warning, famine has visited countries as diverse as Ireland and India, Ethiopia and China. Indeed, despite the near-tripling of the world grain harvest since 1950 the hungry and malnourished in 1998 number an estimated 840 million—nearly as many people as lived in the world when Malthus penned his essay.

But the nature of famine has changed. Whereas it was once geographically defined by areas of poor harvests, today famine is economically defined by low incomes in those segments of society that lack the purchasing power to buy enough food. Famine concentrated among the poor is less visible than the more traditional version but is no less real.

In addition to checks imposed by food shortages, there is evidence that other checks on population growth are now emerging, such as new infectious diseases, including AIDS, Ethnic conflicts within societies, such as Rwanda and the Sudan, are also taking a growing toll. Water shortages on a scale that would deprive people of enough water to produce food could undermine governments.

The evidence gathered here indicates that the rapid population growth prevailing in a majority of the world's countries is not going to continue much longer. Either countries will get their act together, shifting quickly to smaller families, or death rates will rise from one or more of the stresses just mentioned. As human demands press against more and more of the Earth's limits, the questions is not whether population growth will slow, but how. Will it be because countries do it humanely by shifting quickly to smaller families? Or because they fail to do so, and nature ruthlessly imposes its own constraints? In a world facing many challenges as it prepares to enter the next century, this may be the most challenging of all.

Estimates of future numbers are based on the latest United Nations population projections, using their medium level figures. Under this scenario, world population will grow from 6.1 billion in 2000 to 9.4 billion in 2050—a gain of 3.3 billion. The other two U.N. projections put global population in 2050 as high as 11.2 billion or as low as 7.7 billion. While the medium scenario is judged by the U.N. demographers as the one most likely to materialize, it is not an inevitable population part for the next century. Indeed, because the projections are based exclusively on demographic assumptions and do not take into account the environmental limits to carrying capacity, they should be viewed as a first pass rather than the final word on estimates of future population.

We use the medium-level projections to give an idea of the strain this "most likely" outcome would place on ecosystems and governments, and the urgent need to break from the business-as-usual scenario. The mid-level projected growth in population of 3.3 billion by 2050 is very close to the growth that will have occurred between 1950 and 2000, some 3.6 billion. But there is one difference. During the half-century now ending, the growth occurred in both industrial and developing countries. During the next half-century, the entire burden of the projected increase of 3.3 billion will be on developing countries, many of which are hard-pressed to satisfy even existing demands on resources. In fact, the population of the industrial world is expected to decline slightly.

The annual rate of world population growth reached its historical high in 1964 at 2.2 per cent. Since then, it has been slowly declining, dropping to 1.4 per cent in 1998 Despite the falling rate of growth the number of people aged each year increased from 72 million in 1964 to the all-time peak of 87 million in 1990. Since then the annual addition has also declined, falling to 80 million in 1997, where it is projected to remain for the next two decades before starting to decline.

The population projections for individual countries vary more widely than at any time in history. At mid-century populations were growing every where, but today they have stabilised in some 32 countries, while they continue to expand in some countries at 3 per cent or more a year. Indeed, the world can be divided demographically into two camps: countries that have achieved population stability or are well on the way to doing so, and those that have not.

With the exception of Japan, all the nations in the first camp are in Europe, and all are industrial countries. The populations of some countries, including Russia, Japan, and Germany, are actually projected to decline somewhat over the next half-century. In addition to the 32 countries, containing 12 per cent of world population, that have stabilised their populations, in another 39 countries fertility has dropped to replacement level (roughly two children per couple) or below. Among the countries in this category are China and the United States the first and third largest countries, which together contain 26 per cent of the world's people.

Although fertility in these 39 countries has fallen below replacement level, their populations have not yet stabilised because there is a disproportionately large number of young people moving into the reproductive age group. Thus even if they hold their fertility at replacement level, population may continue to grow for several decades before it stabilizes. It was this realisation that led China nearly 20 years ago to shift its goal from two-children to one-child family. Leaders in Beijing realised that, if they did not do this they would be faced with adding the equivalent of another India to their population—a development they considered potentially disastrous for their people.

In contrast to this group some countries are projected to triple their populations over the next half-century. For example, Ethiopia's current population of 62 million will more than triple, as it climbs to 213 million in 2050, Pakistan's population is projected to go from 148 million to 357 million, surpassing that of the United States before 2050 today to 339 million, giving it more people in 2050 than there were in all of Africa in 1950. From an environmental vantage point, considering particularly the availability of water and cropland, it is unlikely that the projected population increases for these three countries, and other countries with similar projected gains, will materialise.

As hard as it is to imagine the addition of another 3.3 billion people to the world's population, it is even more difficult to understand the effects of adding such numbers. As we look back over the last half-century, we see that World lumber use more than doubled, paper use increased nearly six-fold, grain consumption nearly tripled, water use tripled, and fossil fuel burning increased some four-fold. The relative contribution of population growth and rising affluence to the growth in demand for various resources varies widely. With lumber use, most of the doubled use is accounted for by population growth. With paper, in contrast, rising affluence is primarily responsible for the growth in use.

One way to understand the consequences of future population growth is to contrast some of the key trend projected for the next half-century with those of the as one. For example, we have seen a new five-fold growth in the oceanic fish catch and a doubling in the supply available per person, but biologists now believe we may have "hit the wall" in oceanic fisheries and that the oceans cannot sustain a catch any larger than today's. Thus people born today are likely to see the catch per person cut in half during their lifetimes.

Grainland per person has been shrinking since mid-century, but the drop projected for the next 50 years means the world will have less grainland per person than India has today. Future population growth is likely to reduce this key number in many societies to the point where they will no longer be enable to feed themselves. Countries such as Ethiopia, India, Nigeria, and Pakistan will see grainland per person shrink by 2050 to less than one-tenth of a hectare (one-forth of an acre)—far smaller than a typical suburban building lot in the United States.

Given that at the amount of fresh water produced each year is essentially fixed by nature, the water available, per person has shrunk steadily as a result of population growth, leading to severe water shortages in some areas. Countries now experiencing these shortages include China and India, along with scores of smaller ones. As irrigation water is diverted to industrial and residential uses.

The challenge to governments presented by continuing rapid population growth is not limited to natural resources. It also includes education, housing, and jobs. During the last half-century the world has fallen further and further behind in creating jobs, leading to record levels of unemployment and under-employment. Unfortunately over the next 50 years the number of entrants into the job market will be even greater. Few things threaten the political stability of a country as much as growing ranks of unemployed young people.

As noted earlier, the U.N. population projections cited here are based on exclusively demographic assumptions, which are not related to the population carrying capacity of local ecosystems. These projections are purely statistical, based on historical data on fertility, mortality, and average lifespan and assumptions about future trends.

Based on the analysis in it, I conclude that the medium projection of 9.4 billion people in 2050 which U.N. demographers consider to be the most problem is unlikely to materialize. Rather the world is more likely to follow a path closer to the low population projection of 7.7 billion by mid-century.

What is less clear is whether we will move to the lower trajectory because countries with rapid pollution growth quickly shift to smaller families or because they fail to do so and the resulting inability to manage threats from disease, spreading hunger, or social disintegration leads to rising death rates.

35

Aid Effectiveness as a Multi-level Process

Parallel to the widespread decrease of aid resources provided by donor countries to developing countries in recent years, debate and research on how to make aid more effective has become a major concern. Usually, it is suggested that decades of development assistance have at best produced marginal results in terms of improving development levels in the South. Little mention is made of donor's policy shortcomings and the negative impact of these on efforts aimed at reforming and redefining development cooperation in order to enhance aid effectiveness. The policy parameters and operating frameworks of existing aid policies continue to inhibit higher degrees of aid effectiveness. In many donor countries, opinion polls indicate waning public support for development aid.

Increasingly, the moral case for aid is called into question and deeper world market integration tends to be seen as the panacea to continued economic decline and social destabilisation in the South. Against this background, cooperation between donor and recipient actors is faced with a duel uphill struggle. First, fewer resources can be mobilised to meet growing developmental needs. On the other hand, to organise and manage development policies and programmes in a result-oriented manner, grows more difficult. The threat of further aid cuts and of further drops of public support for providing aid become ever more real. A closer look at the organisational complexities and political constraints under which development cooperation is expected to perform effectively may help to improve current aid management approaches.

Towards Conceptual Clarity

At first sight, catchy definitions of what constitutes effective aid might appear attractive to use, in particular with regard to economic indicators. The term "aid effectiveness" is easily used in the same vein as "efficiency", "significance" or "impact" of aid. At times, obsession to measure and demonstrate the results of aid supported development processes can be observed among policy-makers and administrators on the donor side. Still the understanding of aid and its effectiveness as being part and parcel of a cooperation relationship between donor and recipient side parties, is scarcely embedded in practice. To determine how to make aid more effective requires more than a quick impact analysis of an individual and perhaps even isolated development project. Consequently, defining the concept of aid effectiveness needs to take into account at what levels cooperation is focused on. To strive for sustainable and effective modes of development cooperation will entail the need to combine recipient ownership of the development process with donor accountability concerns.

Performance expectations cannot be exclusively placed on the recipient while donor interests, their aid management systems and procedures remain unchanged.

An extended and more analytical, process-oriented definition should take into account four main aspects of aid effectiveness:

(a) Effective aid must relate to the building and/or strengthening of in-country aid management capacity;

(b) To maximise the degree of aid effectiveness, local ownership of the aid process is essential: from setting of priorities through policy formulation and implementation on to the evaluation stages of the process;

(c) Increasing recipient side capabilities to take charge of aid relationship, will need to be combined with arrangements to meet legitimate donor accountability concerns;

(d) Aid effectiveness is a two-faceted objective: its realisation is equally dependent on increased transparency of donor motives and on dropping of non-developmental, political and economic aid objectiveness of donors.

In addition a broader range of stakeholders in the aid relationship needs to be actively involved: extending beyond accountable government and implementing agencies, to include democratic institutions and organisations of civil society and of the private sector.

Applying any definition of aid effectiveness without disaggregating macro-economic data and taking into account country specificity will only lead to unhelpful generalisations about aid and its effectiveness. It would seem more appropriate to adopt working definitions against which to assess effectiveness of aid resources at a country-specific level. On such a basis one could expect to arrive at more reliable indicators of how well aid resources contribute to improving developmental standards and meeting existing needs.

From Definition to Success—Key Requirements

Having reached agreement between the recipient and donor on what should constitute effectiveness of aid is only a starting point. Embarking on democratic, peaceful and participatory patterns of economic and social development must follow: to arrive at significant and lasting improvement in many of the least developed countries will be a long-term process. This being said, it is crucial to design and implements such forms of development cooperation which involve a wide range of recipient side actors, not only from the government side but also from civil society at large. Seen as a process of increasing inclusion of intended beneficiaries of aid, the commitment to decentralise as well as entrust aid and its management grows in importance.

To fully capture Third World development realities, policy frameworks inspired by neoliberalist-type of development concepts and theories are grossly inadequate. The views and positions on aid articulated in the World Bank and the IMF, or in many if not most bilateral aid administrations in OECD countries, represent only one side of today's international cooperation, namely the donor side. The major weakness to point out with respect to this locus of debate, is a profound under representation if not even a total absence of recipient experiences and perceptions on aid in general and on its effectiveness in particular. There-should be little doubt that ignoring to not actively identifying and involving such perceptions, leads to strongly donor driven aid.

To circumvent recipient side insights and views on strengths and weaknesses of aid strategies and mechanisms, will result in limited local commitment and sense of ownership over the aid process. Mutual decision-making between donors and recipients remains a rare policy approach. Aid procedures that are based on local management and less control-oriented donor roles in the aid process are still exceptions in development cooperation.

Structurally, in terms of the policy environment within which development aid is expected to function, the overriding policy framework is general based on structural adjustment policies (SAP). But the underlying conclusion made by proponents of SAPs that these policies induce aid effectiveness, has yet to be proven valid. It must suffice at this point to emphasize that there is no *a priori* relationship between world market integration under structural adjustment and sustainable development in poor countries. Aid to these countries which is solely intended to reinforce fundamentally uneven and unequal patterns of world market integration should be scrutinised critically.

Some central issues need to be addressed in the course of improving aid and its effectiveness:

- institutional dimensions of aid relationships require strong policy-attention, both on the donor and the recipient side;
- capacities to effectively identify and formulate aid priorities need to be strengthened in recipient countries;
- local capacities to sustain reform efforts must be reinforced.

Levels of Intervention

If the design of aid and the terms upon which it is provided to a developing country are largely determined by the donor, the aid relationship can be characterised as essentially hierarchical. Recipient side views will rarely surface, as they are either not identified, or not well formulated. Possibilities of a recipient-led development strategies can be limited. Unless scope is provided to the recipient side actors to assume responsibilities, aid effectiveness is likely to remain low or fluctuating, and the sustainability of donor aid efforts will remain doubtful.

National planning processes and courses of national development in recipient countries should be seen as most effective where they are led under local responsibility and control. To arrive at this ideal situation, gaps need to be reduced and closed at the various intervention levels.

Donor aid resources provide valuable support for this process. Their effectiveness in meeting long-term objective of aid will need to be assessed on the basis of how well they perform at the different levels. Individual donors will expectedly perform differently at the various levels. What will prove to be the ultimate test for effectiveness is how well the donor aid performance accomplishes the broader objectives of development cooperation and how well it includes sustainable results.

In the analytical frameworks outlined here, development cooperation would seem to be confronted with the effectiveness gaps at the:

- *Structural Level:* International trade and investment patterns, debt problems and world market integration process appear as long-term constraining factors upon aid and its effectiveness;
- *Policy Level:* Dialogue and partnership in development cooperation are instrumental factors in recluding planning and co-ordination gaps with regard to policy analysis and formulation;
- *The Institutional Level* is where pertinent capacity gaps exist: capacity development efforts of donors and technical assistance measures play an important role in addressing weaknesses in aid effectiveness within a country's institutional setting;
- Finally, at the *level of aid projects* (programmes), it is generally the lack of sustainability of aid interventions which causes development activities to falter once donor support decreases or stops. In addition to technical cooperation, financial and material inputs serve to maintain project momentum and goal realisation. The issue of how to develop local capacity sufficiently in order for indigenous organisations to continue project activities initially supported by donor aid, remains the most important issue to address at this level.

Fostering Aid Effectiveness

Donor and recipient development efforts are too often isolated from one another, or poorly coordianted. They fail to address managerial and implementation bottlenecks. Cross-sectoral linkages, as well as interdisciplinary approaches to aid problems are only slowly gaining ground. It is increasingly obvious, that decisions on aid issues are subjected to concerns outside of the responsible ministry. Finance Ministers, and unfortunately even Defence Ministers have a strong say in how much aid is to be provided, where it is to be concentrated and under what terms to be utilised. Inside of recipient countries, large portions of national budgets are allocated to non-development priorities with little or no impact on alleviating urgent poverty problems.

Development cooperation may make the biggest impact and be executed most effectively where donors and recipients agree upon multi-level aid strategies. To give an example, building a road to a remote rural area may well be done in an effective project manner. It is equally important to have a functioning transport authority in place to ensure maintenance of the roads. If this authority operates within a nationally defined infrastructure policy, best in accord with national trade and investment priorities, then the effectiveness of the project-level road building programme has a good chance of being high.

Institutional changes to set the stage for a profound reform process in development cooperation are needed. Reprioritising national budgets to reflect identified in country development needs may be one step. Setting up policy evaluation and formulation units can be complimentary measures. Deregulating markets and investment rules may serve to please donors, but dumping of cheap products which strangle local production efforts may easily result. Regional cooperation, including intensified South-South cooperation can provide some counterbalance. There are only a few areas where changes in the current system of development cooperation can occur, with a view to better manage the complexities of aid and the social, cultural, economic and political backgrounds against which they take place. The will and commitment to take policy action in both donor and recipient countries, through the broadest range of stakeholders and institutions as possible, will be the test for genuine efforts at improving development relations between North and South and organising cooperation effectively.

36

Crisis and New Orientation of Development Policy

The poverty in the South, the dislocations in the East, and the orientation crisis in the North are not isolated phenomena. Rather, they represent an alarming amalgamation of dangers that are globally interlinked.

The low effectiveness of international economic and development policy is rooted in two outdated paradigms on which the present worldwide strategy of economic development is based, namely that:

1. The Western social and economic model optimizes the activation of productive forces—independent of the development stage of a country and its culture and therefore is best suited to satisfy basic needs.

2. It is possible to launch the development of a society from the outside within a few decades—without regard to its cultural and historical background—through external input of money, goods, technology, expertise, and personnel.

The twin paradigms of the timelessness and transferability combined with cultural ecological, and financial restrictions—have led international cooperation and development down the wrong path.

Only if we acknowledge the true dimensions of the global dangers, if we recognise the limitations and shortcomings of existing political instruments, and identify outdated theories and contradictory special interests, can we outline the cornerstones of a new policy of global cooperation.

Cornerstones of a New Development Policy

Starting with critical review of the shortcomings and paradigms of the prevailing development strategy, the following ten cornerstones of a new development policy are offered for discussion:

1. *Broaden the Concept of Development*

Whether a society is considered developed depends on the size of its per capita Gross National Product (GNP). Accordingly, the world is divided into a developed, semi-developed, and underdeveloped world. The yardstick for development, which has become the norm in the industrial countries, is one-dimensional. It only measures the monetary value of goods and services that are exchanged in the marketplace. This standard is too narrow economically because it compresses the multitude and complexity of cultural, societal, historical, social, and human values into a single economic category.

At the most, there can and should be agreement on what development and progress should not bring about. Inability to find enough work to meet the most basic needs; exploitation and oppression of people; loss of cultural wealth and institutions; destruction of natural resources. These, however, are the very values that are sacrificed by the prevailing development strategy. In the future, development policy must do all it can to stop the loss of skills and self-reliance, the plunder of natural resources, the erosion of cultural values, the violation of human dignity and human rights. Initiatives must prevail which are orientated on these values, and not just on the GNP.

2. *Concentrate Development Strategy on the Internal Potential of Developing Countries*

There must be an end to the manic fixation of development strategy on external inputs and external markets. A new development policy must, above all, improve internal conditions for a productive economy, promote domestic production factors on a broad basis, protect cultural and natural resources, and greatly increase the domestic supply of basic goods. Wherever external inputs are unavoidable, credits must be strictly tied to the productivity and the ability of a country to absorb transfers. External transfers should be concentrated on "Software" for health, education, social participation, administrative, and legal jurisdiction. Such an approach could also promote training and indigenous technologies, which are so important for economic development.

The set-up and expansion of the productive sectors must be decided, planned and implemented by the developing countries themselves, and they must assume full responsibility. The external pressures, which force the developing countries into full integration with the world market, must be removed. This presupposes a structural reduction of interest rates.

3. *Make Development Policy a Central Feature of Politics*

Development policy must take the lead in mobilizing the various political forces and government departments to join the fight against the growing global dangers. It must ensure that the actions of all political departments are compatible with development policy is possible only if it becomes the central task of all political sectors, comparable to social and environmental policies, and the central goal of all policies. If development policy is to become a central task, development problems must become a priority in parliament and government. Society must understand that it is in the national interest to accept great global responsibilities.

4. *Reform the World Economy*

The industrial countries must abolish their protectionism in agriculture as well the processed goods sector. Simultaneously, the developing countries need to be protected selectively and for a limited time against imports from the industrial countries. The undifferentiated structural adjustment policies imposed by the IMF must be revised. The trend toward regionalisation of the world economy should not be opposed; rather, in the interest of both South and East, it must be regulated constructively to form a new, regionally based world trade structure.

A reform of the international finance system is urgently needed. Interest and exchange rates should not mirror the national interests of the big industrial states and the special interests of large banks and venture capital. Rather, they must reflect the global interest in monetary stability lower and stable interest rates, and sufficient development financing.

However, strengthening the international financial institutions is in the global interest only if the countries of the southern and eastern hemispheres are allowed to exert some influence. An international financial court must guarantee that violations of strict regulations to ensure international stability and solvency can be protested in a court of law.

5. *Redesign the Industrial Society*

As a global social and environmental policy, the new development policy must induce the industrial countries to give up their excessive consumption of air, water, soil, resources, and space. Increased utilisation of energy-conservation measures and environmentally friendly technologies is overdue. The economic and social policies of the industrial nations must promote balance rather than growth. This requires radical changes in traditional economic thinking, habits, structures and processes.

In view of limited world resources, unsatisfied existential needs in South and East, and continuous population growth in the South, the only premise for the future can be. Growth rates in the South must be higher than in the North, but they should no longer be in the North, but they should no longer be induced primarily by growth in the North. If economic policies continue to call for the North to provide the locomotive, the North will have to continue to acquire more resources than the South.

The North must relinquish the remaining growth frontiers to the South and East. The South must use this opportunity to activate its internal dynamic potential rather than integrate its economy with the North. However, ecological and social controls must be established at a much earlier stage than was the case in Europe.

6. *Strengthen Development Cooperation*

The share of official development assistance as a percentage of GNP, which dropped from 0.48 per cent in 1982 to 0.34 per cent in 1995 must be gradually raised again and reach at least 0.7 per cent in the year 2000—a goal which OECD established as early as two decades ago and which was reconfirmed at the Rio Earth Summit.

However, we must not succumb to the illusion that a doubling of ODA funds will even remotely meet the financial needs of South and East. State development policy must use its scarce public funds more effectively in the future. It must use restraint whenever partners in the developing countries can accomplish a task on their own and private initiatives and private enterprise are more competent to do the job. The government should be directly engaged only when it can be relatively more productive. Otherwise, it should limit itself to subsidizing private organisations.

7. *New Orientation for Development Cooperation*

The state and its implementation agencies must abandon all direct responsibility for any projects which require unbureaucratic action, economic efficiency, and long-term productivity. It must make a much greater effort to involve NGO's and private venture capital in development projects. At the same time, the state must insist and guarantee that private actions are compatible with social and ecological concerns.

In the future, the main thrust of government projects should be the promotion of the internal potential of a country. This comprises the political and administrative framework conditions of a humane, socially and ecologically sound development. Constitutional government, social institutions which facilitate broad participation of the population in politics, society, and economy; efficient savings, credit, fiscal and financial systems; mechanisms for income, property, and land distribution which promote productivity, justice, and social peace. In addition of this "software" of development, the following is needed: A regimen for the protection of resources and environment; measures to prevent the short-term sell out of natural resources; elementary and general education and training, healthcare and social safety nets; capacities to develop science and technology.

8. *Reduce the Debt Service and Activate Private Capital*

Public funds must be used to a greater degree for the financial rehabilitation of highly indebted countries in South and East; external demands for interest and principal payments must be adapted to the economic capacity of the respective country and its ability to execute external capital transfers.

Within the framework of international insolvency regulations, initiatives must be developed as a condition for the continuance of the present rules for write-offs which ensure effective cooperation from the banks and alleviate the heavy burden of private credits, with their high interest rates.

State development policy and private business interests should supplement each other. Government promotion of private enterprise initiatives for exports, investment, and employment in the developing countries must take into account their compatibility with development. In reverse, private engagements that effectively promote development must be actively supported by the government. A separate line item must be established in the development budget for such activation of private capital.

9. *Set Regional Priorities*

State development cooperation has been scattering its scarce funds not only among too many sectors, but also among too many partners. In the future, public funds must be concentrated regionally. More emphasis must be placed on regional programmes, and development cooperation with threshold countries must be enhanced. A portion of public funds should be set aside to provide an incentive for threshold countries to assist the poorer nations in their own region as well as deal with poverty in their own country.

The new development policy could then also help lessen ethnic-national conflicts and promote peace by sponsoring regional cooperation in joint development projects. For this purpose, regional development funds must be set up for cooperation in the transportation, energy, trade, and finance sectors and last, but not least for regional security systems and disarmament. Such regional funds could also provide the means to project refugees and improve their prospects for an eventual return to their homelands.

37

Technological Entrepreneurship

The New Force for Economic Growth

Entrepreneurship has emerged as a major new force for change. The dynamic role of modern small business in economic growth has received fresh recognition worldwide. It is essential to promote entrepreneurship and to mobilise the dynamism of the private sector for accelerated national development. An unbridled private sector may not, however, ensure growth with equity. It is the prime responsibility of governments to create policy frameworks that enable businesses to apply technology for competitive advantage and for the well-being of the public.

The Changing Global Environment

As agents of change and progress, entrepreneurs start by identifying a market opportunity and matching this with social or technical innovations. They then proceed to mobilise the resources necessary to drive their business concept to its commercial realisation. The development of a product or service with a high-technology content—never easy anywhere, or at today's rapidly-changing global environment. It calls for restructuring the available technology and business development systems and developing the skills needed by a new breed of "techno-entrepreneurs" to transform innovations into market opportunities at home and abroad. It also requires reorienting the present processes and priorities of technical and economic cooperation among countries.

Amidst the global concerns of environmental preservation, poverty elimination and social development, the practical problems of entrepreneurship are not being properly addressed, even though entrepreneurs will create the bulk of enterprises, jobs and wealth.

A torrent of technology-based goods hits the market every week, ostensibly improving the quality of our lives while simultaneously creating complexity and dislocation. The pace of progress in information technologies, micro-electronics, robotics, new materials, biomedical sciences, space science and other advanced technologies quickens, significantly changing the way we live. The growth of markets for these technologies also proceeds apace.

Further, technological change is taking place today against a background of growing intra-national and international disequilibria. While the transformation from state-centred to market-oriented development is opening up enormous opportunities and options, it has also caused severe short-term hardships. In order to survive and prosper in these changing times, India and its enterprises need enlightened government policies, good technical infrastructure and strong cultural roots.

Traditional production factors are giving way to a new paradigm characterised by new patterns of trade, investment and employment, and by informal networking life-long learning and technological entrepreneurship. The manufacturing sector in India continues to be dominated by food products, textiles, chemicals and other traditional industry, mainly in the public sector. However, change is coming, albeit slowly. State enterprises are being corporatised pending privatisation, and the share of knowledge-based and information-related activities in the marketplace is rising perceptibly. Restructuring policies now place emphasis (often purely rhetorical) on the role of the private sector. The legacy of decades of centrally-planned development is generally inimical to private enterprise. In turn, the private sector has been slow to respond to economic liberalisation in India and generally failed to generate the new employment necessary to absorb new entrants to the labour force.

The regulatory problems of an onerous tax structure and administration, poor access to finance and raw materials, over-regulation of labour and land-use, pervasive bureaucracy and restricted markets have been significant barriers to entrepreneurial growth.

Towards Competitive Performance

The imperative of improved performance has serious implications for India if it is to survive, stay abreast and succeed. It calls for national efforts on systemic efficiency and productivity growth, the move from an investment-driven to an innovation-driven economy and sustained higher-order competitiveness; towards enhanced customer satisfaction at home and penetration of selected markets abroad. Concurrently, governments and business have to address such intractable problems as poverty, corruption and the degradation of the environment.

Creating New Technology-based Ventures

Starting a new business in India is a hazardous task. Problems are compounded when the venture is technology-based:

- Capital requirements are generally larger, while traditional banks are ill-equipped to process the perceived risk. Venture capital generally only becomes an option when the venture has documented the merits of its management, market and innovation.
- Knowledge-based ventures can benefit from linkages to sources of knowledge, e.g. the technical university or research lab. Such mentoring needs to be cultivated.
- Techno-entrepreneurs often have technical skills but usually lack the business management and marketing skills necessary for success. These need to be supplemented.

- In fields where technology is changing rapidly, it is often advantageous to make technology-acquisition arrangements. Sourcing such innovations, negotiating technology licensing agreements and protecting the intellectual property itself require special skills.
- Knowledge-based innovations are inherently more risky than others. The management of this unique risk requires assessment techniques and vision.
- Technology-based ventures often have social and environmental implications, which need to be managed carefully.
- Penetrating a competitive market requires good market intelligence, a good strategic plan and good luck.

Special Characteristics of "Techno-entrepreneurs"

The popular misconceptions are that techno-entrepreneurs are born, not made; that they take risks with other people's money and fail more often than they succeed. In fact, entrepreneur skills can be identified and developed. The entrepreneur is typically an innovator who formulates new solutions to existing problems, mobilises resources and stimulates others to participate in his or her team. These aptitudes develop over time, often starting in childhood, as the person faces new challenges and learns from failure.

Entrepreneurial opportunities can be found in every industrialising country, community and family. Principal sources of entrepreneurs for knowledge-based ventures are often the university and government research laboratories, the large industrial and military establishments and professional service firms. Some motivations of the entrepreneur are the need to be independent; create value; contribute to society; earn recognition; become rich or; quite often, simply not to be unemployed. Value-adding ventures with good growth potential can best be developed in an open market and in a culture which supports risk-taking.

The techno-entrepreneur anywhere has the challenge of moving a concept through the prototype and production phases towards creation of a product which meets market needs at a price consistent with the value created and with the ability of customers to pay.

Equally important, the market itself has to be developed and sustained. It is not enough to be first with a better mousetrap if one does not have the skills to educate and reach potential buyers and to set the market standard.

Hence one has to distinguish between innovators and inventors. The inventor is typically a creative person in a quest for knowledge or for producing new products, without determining in advance whether a real market exists for his or her inventions. On the other hand, the innovator draws on existing knowledge and the talents of others to develop or adapt a product or service at a volume and cost that can capture a significant portion of an identified market. The flexibility and creativity of a small entrepreneurial techno-venture may lead to more incremental and break-through innovations than can be generated by larger-sized firms in many sectors.

The pace and pattern of India's economic development now depend in large measure on its technical resource base. In this context, the key determinants are the skills to apply technology for enhanced competitiveness, as well as to create tech-based ventures. Techno-entrepreneurs have to be supported by appropriate national structures and international linkages if they are to survive and flourish in an intensely competitive world.

38

The Truth About Global Competition

The Economic Myths Behind Globalisation

Local communities everywhere are on the front lines of what might well be characterised as World War III. It is not the nuclear confrontation between East and West—between the Soviet Union and the United States—that we once feared. It is a very different kind of conflict. There is no clash of competing military forces and the struggle is not defined by national borders. But it does involve an often violent struggle for control of physical resources and territory that is destroying lives and communities at every hand. It is a struggle between the forces and institutions of economic globalisation and the communities that are trying to reclaim control of their economic lives. It is a conflict between competing goals—economic growth to maximize profits for absentee owners versus creating healthy communities that are good places for people to live. It is a competition for the control of markets and resources between global corporations and financial markets on the one hand and locally owned businesses serving local markets on the other.

Two things of fundamental importance to each and every one of us are now very much at stake.

- Will people and communities control their local resources and economies and be able to set their own goals and priorities based on their own values and aspiration? Or will these decisions be left to global financial markets and corporations that are blind to all values save one—instant financial returns?

- Will the life sustaining resources produced by the regenerative capacities of our planet's ecosystems be equitably shared to provide for the material needs of all of us who inhabit this bountiful planet, as well as for our children and their children unto the seventh generation and beyond? Or will we allow a global economic system that is now functioning on auto-pilot beyond conscious human control to consume and destroy the ecosystem and our social fabric in its insatiable quest for money?

Economists, politicians, corporate spokespersons and the media have for years been touting the benefits of the global economy. They have called on us to support trade agreements such as the North American Free Trade Agreement (NAFTA) and the World Trade Organisation (WTO) to remove the constraints of economic borders and open to everyone the opportunities of growth and prosperity in the global economy. They have promised rich rewards for those workers and communities that become successful global competitors.

Many of the most ardent boosters of economic globalisation met earlier in the year at the annual meeting of the World Economic Forum. This Forum has for years brought together top industrialists and political figures from around the world to advance the proposition that removing tariffs and other restrictions on the free international flow of trade and money is a key to creating new economic opportunity and prosperity. It thus caused quite a stir when the Forum publicly announced that economic globalisation is producing disastrous consequences that threaten the political stability of the Western democracies. Their warning bears close examination for being one of the most honest and accurate assessments of the consequences of economic globalisation yet produced by leading advocates of that process. The observation is that:

- Economic globalisation is causing severe economic dislocation and social instability.
- The technological changes of the past few years have eliminated more jobs than they have created.
- The global competition "that is part and parcel of globalisation leads to winner-take-all situations; those who come out on top win big, and the losers lose even bigger."
- Higher profits no longer mean more job security and better wages. "Globalisation tends to delink the fate of the corporation from the fate of its employees."
- Unless serious corrective action is taken soon, the backlash could destabilize the Western democracies.

We don't have to go far to find examples of what they are talking about and why people are getting a bit upset as they wake up to the realities of who is winning in the ruthless competition of the global economy. The disparities between the winners and losers in the global competition are becoming more obscene with each passing day.

We are coming to realize that the extravagant promises of the advocates of the global economy are based on a number of myths that have become so deeply embedded in Western industrial culture that we have grown to accept them without examination.

- The myth that growth in GNP is a valid measure of human well being and progress.
- The myth that free unregulated markets efficiently allocate a society's resources.
- The myth that growth in trade benefits ordinary people
- The myth that global corporations are benevolent institutions that if freed from governmental

interference will provide a clean environment for all and good jobs for the poor.

- The myth that absentee investors create local prosperity.

The Growth Myth

Our measures of growth are deeply flawed in that they are purely measures of activity in the monetised economy. Expanded use of cigarettes and alcohol increases economic output both as a direct consequence of their consumption and because of the related increase in health care needs. The need to clean up oil spills generates economic activity. Gun sales to minors generate economic activity. A divorce generates both lawyers fees and the need to buy or rent and outfit a new home increasing real estate brokerage fees and retail sales. It is now well documented that in number of other countries the quality of living of ordinary people has been declining as aggregate economic output increases.

The growth myth has another serious flaw. Since 1950, the world's economic output has increased 5 to 7 times. That growth has already increased the human burden on the planet's regenerative systems—its soils, air, water, fisheries, and forestry systems—beyond what the planet can sustain. Continuing to press for economic growth beyond the planet's sustainable limits does two things. It accelerates the rate of breakdown of the earth's regenerative systems—as we see so dramatically demonstrated in the case of many ocean fisheries, and it intensifies the competition between rich and poor for the resource base that remains.

This is vividly illustrated by many of the development projects in India many funded with loans from the World Bank and other multilateral development banks—that displace the poor so that the lands and waters on which they depend for their livelihood can be converted to uses that generate higher economic returns—meaning converted to use by people who can pay more than those who are displaced.

The Myth of Free Unregulated Markets

It is almost inherent in the nature of markets that their efficient function depends on the presence of a strong government to set a framework of rules for their operation. We know that free markets create monopolies, which government must break up to maintain the conditions of competition on which market function depends.

We also know that markets only allocate efficiently when prices reflect the full and true costs of production. Yet in the absence of governmental regulation, market incentives persistently push firms to cut corners on safety, pay workers less than a living wages, and dump untreated toxic discharges into a convenient river. In our present competitive context if management does not take such measures, they are likely to be replaced by the owners or bought out by someone with less scruples who will.

The Myth of Free Trade

Many so-called trade agreements, such as the North American Free Trade Agreement (NAFTA) and the World Trade Organisation (WTO) are not really trade agreements at all. They are economic integration agreements intended to guarantee the rights of global corporations to move both goods and investments wherever they wish—free from public interference and accountability. WTO is best described as a bill of rights for global corporations.

The Myth that Economic Globalisation is Inevitable

Many of the people who claim globalisation is a consequence of inevitable historical forces are paid to promote that message by the same global corporations that have invested millions of dollars in advancing the globalisation policy agenda.

The Myth that Corporations are Benevolent Institutions

The corporation is an institutional invention specifically and internationally created to concentrate control over economic resources while shielding those who hold the resulting power from liability for the consequences of its use. The more national economies become integrated into a seamless global economy, the further corporate power extends beyond the reach of any state and the less accountable it becomes to any human interest or institution other than a global financial system that is now best described as a gigantic legal gambling casino.

All over the world people are indeed waking up to the truth about economic globalisation and are taking steps to reclaim and rebuild their local economies. Such communities face basic choices as to how they will divide their efforts between competing for a share of the declining pool of good jobs that global corporations offer and working to create locally owned enterprises that sustainably harvest and process local resources to produce the jobs and the goods and services that local people need to live healthy, happy, and fulfilling lives in balance with the environment.

Our experience with the real consequences of economic globalisation is pointing to many important lessons. One such lesson is that economies should be local, rooting power in the people and communities who realize their well-being depends on the health and vitality of their local ecosystem. If it is protectionist to favour local firms and workers who pay local taxes, live by local rules, respect and nurture the local ecosystems, compete fairly in local markets, and contribute to community life—then let us all proudly proclaim ourselves to be protectionist.

Such choices are not isolationist. To the contrary, they create a foundation for creative cooperation with our neighbours—whether they be in the United States or in other countries—to share experience, ideas and technology—and to join in international solidarity in rewriting the rules of the global economy to favour local over global businesses, and to encourage cooperative relations among people and communities. It is our consciousness—our ways of thinking and our sense of membership in a larger community—not our economies—that should be global.

Millions of people are also making an important discovery that life is about living-not consuming. A life of material sufficiency can be filled with social, cultural, intellectual, and spiritual abundance that place no burden on the planet.

It is time to assume responsibility for creating a new human future of just and sustainable communities freed from the myth that greed, competition, and mindless consumption are paths to individual and collective fulfillment. It will take millions of people around the world—linked together into a powerful political coalition aimed at radical, political and economic—reform to win the war that global capital is waging against us.

Bibliography

De Soto, H., 1990. *The Other Path; The Invisible Revolution in the Third World,* Reprint edition. New York: Harper Collins.

Doha Development Agenda, 2001. *The Ministerial Declaration and other Decisions and Declarations from the Doha Ministerial Conference,* Available: http://www.wto,org/english/tratop_e/dda_e/dda_e.htm.

English, P., B. Hoekman, and A. Mattoo, 2002, *Development, Trade and the WTO: A Handbook.* The World Bank, Washington, D.C.

Feketekuty, G., 1988. *International Trade in Services: An Overview and Blueprint for Negotiations,* Cambridge, MA: American Enterprise Institute/Ballinger.

Finger, J.M., 1993. *Antidumping: How It Works and Who Gets Hurt.* Ann Arbor: Univ. of Michigan Press.

Finger, J.M., 2001. "Implementing the Uruguay Round Agreements: Problems for Developing Countries." *The World Economy* 24(9, September): 107-108.

Finger, J.M. and J.J. Nogues, 2001. The Unbalanced Uruguay Round Outcome: The New Areas in Future WTO Negotiations. *Policy Research Working Paper No. 2732,* The World Bank, Washington, D.C.

Finger, J.M. and L. Schuknecht, 2001. "Market Access Advances and Retreats: The Uruguay Round and Beyond." In B. Hoekman and W. Martin, eds., *Developing Countries and the WTO: A Pro-active Agenda.* Oxford: UK and Malden. Also available as Policy Research Working Paper No. 2232 at http://www.worldbank.org/research/trade.

Finger, J.M. and P. Schuler, 2000. "Implementation of Uruguay Round Commitments: The Development Challenge." *The*

World Economy 23(4, April): 511-25. Also available as Policy Research Working Paper No. 2215 at http://www.worldbank.org/research/trade.

Finger, J.M. and L.A. Winters, 2002. "Reciprocity." In P. English, B. Hoekman, and A. Mattoo, *Development, Trade and the WTO: A Handbook.* The World Bank, Washington, D.C.

Finger. J.M., M.D. Ingco, and U. Reincke, 1996. *The Uruguay Round: Statistics on Tariif Concessions Given and Received.* The World Bank, Washington, D.C.

Finger, J.M., F. Ng, and S. Wangchuk, 2001. Antidumping as Safeguard Policy. Policy Research Working Paper No. 2730, The World Bank, Washington, D.C.

Francois, J.F., B. McDonald, and H. Nordstrom, 1996. "The Uruguay Round: A Numerically Based Qualitative Assessment." In W. Martin and L.A. Winters, eds., *The Uruguay Round and the Developing Countries.* Cambridge: Cambridge: University Press.

Harrison, G.W., T.F. Rutherford, and D.G. Tarr, 1996. "Quantifying the Uruguay Round." In W. Martin and L.A. Winters, eds., *The Uruguay Round and the Developing Countries.* Cambridge: Cambridge University Press.

Hudec, R.E., 1970. "The GATT Legal System: A Diplomat's Jurisprudence." *Journal of World Trade Law* 4:615-65.

International Intellectual Property Alliance (IIPA), 2002a. "Description of the IIPA." Available: http://www.iipa.com/aboutiipa.html.

International Intellectual Property Alliance (IIPA), 2002b. "Statistics."Available: http://www.iipa. com/statistics.html.

Martin, W. and L.A. Winters, 1996. *The Uruguay Round and the Developing Countries.* Cambridge; Cambridge University Press.

Martin. W and L.A. Winters, 1996. "The Uruguay Round: a Milestone for the Developing Countries." In W. Martin and L.A. Winters, eds., *The Uruguay Round and the Developing Countries.* Cambridge: Cambridge University Press.

Maskus, K.E., 2000. *Intellectual Property Rights in the Global Economy.* Institute for International Economics, Washington, D.C.

Michalopoulos, C., 1999. "The Developing Countries in the WTO." *The World Economy* 22(1) January.

O'Neill, T. and G. Hymel (contributor), 1995, *All Politics is Local: And Other Rules of the Game*. Reprint edition. Massachusetts: Adams Media Corporation.

Panagariya, A., forthcoming. "Developing Countries at Doha: A Political Economy Analysis." *The World Economy*.

Petersen, M. and D.G. McNeil Jr., 2001. "Maker Yielding Patent in Africa for AIDS Drug" *The New York Times*. 15 March. p. 1.

Preeg, E.H., 1995. *Traders in a Brave New World*. Chicago and London: University of Chicago Press.

Reichman, J.H., 1998. "Securing Compliance with the TRIPS Agreement after US v India." *Journal of International Economic Law* 1(4, December): 603-06.

Ricupero, R., 2000. "A Development Round: Converting Rhetoric into Substance." Paper Presented at the Symposium on Efficiency, Equity and Legitimacy: The Multilateral Trading System at the Millennium, 1-2 June, John F. Kennedy School of Government, Harvard University, Cambridge, Massachusetts.

Shaffer, G., 2002. "The Law-in Action of International Trade Litigation: The Blurring of the Public and the Private." University of Wisconsin Law School, Madison Manuscript.

Winham, G., 1986. *International Trade and The Tokyo Round of Negotiations*. Princeton: Princeton University Press.

Winters, L.A., 2002. "Doha and the World Poverty Targets." Paper Prepared for the Annual Bank Conference on Development Economics (ABCDE), 29-30 April, World Bank, Washington, D.C.

World Bank, 2002, *Global Economic Prospects and the Developing Countries*. The World Bank, Washington D.C.

World Trade Organisation (WTO), 2002a. "WTO Secretariat Budget for 2002." Available: http://www.wto.org/english/thewto_e/secre_e/budget _e.htm.

World Trade Organisation (WTO), 2002b. Pledging Conference to provide sound financial basis for Doha Agenda. Available: http://www.wto.org./english/news_e/pres02_e/pr277_e.htm.

Zeller, T.W., 1992. *American Trade and Power in the 1960s*. New York: Columbia.

Index